SPECIAL

OPS

JOURNAL OF THE ELITE FORCES
& SWAT UNITS
VOL.25

MW00446439

CONCORD
PUBLICATIONS COMPANY

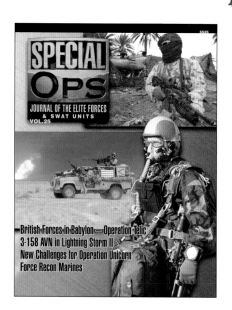

Editor: Samuel M. Katz
Associate Editor: James R. Hill
Copyright © 2003
by CONCORD PUBLICATIONS CO.
603-609 Castle Peak Road
Kong Nam Industrial Building
10/F, B1, Tsuen Wan
New Territories, Hong Kong
www.concord-publications.com

We welcome authors who can help
expand our range of books. If you
would like to submit material, please
feel free to contact us.

We are always on the look-out for
new, unpublished photos for this
series. If you have photos or slides or
information you feel may be useful
to future volumes, please send them
to us for possible future publication.
Full photo credits will be given upon
publication.

ISBN 962-361-065-3
printed in Hong Kong

British Forces in Babylon

"Operation Telic"
The UK's Mission in "Operation Iraqi Freedom"
Samuel M. Katz

A fully armed Land Rover from the 1st Battalion The Royal Irish Regiment advances past an oil well set alight by Iraqi forces near Basra. (Courtesy: UK MoD)

The darkened skies were quiet over Basra, the principal Iraqi outlet to the Persian Gulf, though the sound in the distant offered a telltale hit of thunder. The long-awaited war to oust Saddam Hussein from power was moments away from eruption. The talk had been of "shock and awe," but for the green berets on the ground, veterans of the Royal Marine Commando fraternity of warrior, shock and awe was part and parcel of their operational existence. Their faces adorned in a blackened design of camouflage black, and their eyes utilizing the latest in night-vision technology, the men who proudly sport the Globe and Laurel on their berets were about to yet again assume the vanguard under fire on yet another battlefield so distant from home. The Royal Marines would be the first into the fire—they would be followed by some 40,000 British troops assigned to the Allied war effort in what President George W. Bush had labeled "Operation Iraqi Freedom."

Royal Marines zero in their weapons as they prepare for the assault into Iraq. (Courtesy: UK MoD)

For the United States, the United Kingdom had proven itself—especially in the dark days immediately following the 9/11 al-Qaeda attacks against New York City and Washington D.C., to be an ally second-to-none. Britain was among the first nations to wholly commit its military forces—from the elite shadowy warriors of the SAS to armor and RAF regiments—to fight in "Operation Enduring Freedom" in Afghanistan. The United States pushed for an international coalition to ensure that Iraqi strongman Saddam Hussein would not be able to continue with his desire to amass an arsenal of weapons of mass destruction, and possibly provide these nuclear, chemical and biological agents to terrorists. But America's desire to assemble an international United Nations military bloc to confront Saddam Hussein failed under the dubiously motivated efforts of both the French and Germans—two nations with elaborate economic ties to Saddam Hussein. America, having suffered over nearly 3,000 dead in one horrific mega-attack of its own, was determined to go it alone if the world would not rise to occasion and preemptively deter the Iraqi dictator. Prime Minister Tony Blair was resolute in his determination to separate politics in usual from a tactical decision of right versus wrong and the United Kingdom once again stood shoulder-to-shoulder with her American allies.

Between January 7 and February 6 the United Kingdom deployed a substantial sea, air and land force to bolster American military personnel staging in Qatar and Kuwait for the strike against Iraq. The naval armada consisted of:
- The aircraft carrier HMS *Ark Royal*
- The helicopter carrier HMS *Ocean*
- The Type 42 destroyer HMS *Liverpool*
- The Type 42 destroyer HMS *Edinburgh*
- The Type 42 destroyer HMS *York*
- The Type 23 frigate HMS *Marlborough*
- The Type 23 frigate HMS *Richmond*

In addition to this armada, the United Kingdom also deployed two mine

A Warrior prepares to breach Iraqi positions in the opening phase of the war. (Courtesy: UK MoD)

hunting ships (the HMS *Grimsby* and *HMS Ledbury*) plus a support fleet of other vessels and hospital ships. A fleet submarine, capable of launching cruise missiles, was also deployed.

The amphibious force dispatched to the Iraqi Theater of Operations (ITO) included:
- HQ 3 Commando Brigade
- 40 Commando Royal Marines
- 42 Commando Royal Marines
- Elements of the Special Boat Service (SBS)

British land force sent into the ITO numbered some 26,000 troops and included:

1st Armoured Division
- Headquarters and 1st Armoured Division Signal Regiment
- 30 Signal Regiment (strategic communications)
- The Queen's Dragoon Guards (reconnaissance and long-range tactical field intelligence)
- 1st Battalion The Duke of Wellington's Regiment (light infantry)
- 28 Engineer Regiment
- 1 Regiment, Royal Military Police

In addition to these units, other support and medical regiments and forces were attached to the divisional assets, including:
- 33 Explosive Ordnance Disposal Regiment
- 30 Signal Regiment
- 32 Regiment Royal Artillery (Phoenix UAVs)

7th Armoured Brigade
- Headquarters and Signal Squadron
- Royal Scots Dragoon Guards (Challenger 2 MBTs)
- 2nd Royal Tank Regiment

(Challenger 2 MBTs)
- 1st Battalion The Black Watch (Warrior AIFVs)
- 1st Battalion Royal Regiment of Fusiliers (Warrior AIFVs)
- 3rd Regiment Royal Horse Artillery (AS90 self-propelled artillery)
- 32 Armoured Engineer Regiment

Additional forces attached to the overall 7th Armoured Division umbrella command included:
- Queen's Royal Lancers (Challenger 2 MBTs)
- 1st Battalion Irish Guards (Warrior AIFVs)
- 1st Battalion The Light Infantry (Warrior AIFVs)
- 26 Regiment Royal Artillery
- 38 Engineer Regiment

16 Air Assault Brigade
- Headquarters and Signal Squadron
- 1st Battalion the Royal Irish Regiment

WMIK Land Rovers patrol the no man's land before the war. (Courtesy: UK MoD)

4

A 1st Armoured Division Challenger 2 MBT advances into Iraq from its base of deployment in Kuwait. (Courtesy: UK MoD)

- 1st Battalion The Parachute Regiment
- 3rd Battalion The Parachute Regiment
- 7 (Para) Regiment Royal Horse Artillery (105mm light artillery)
- 23 Engineer Regiment
- Household Cavalry Regiment (armored reconnaissance squadron)
- 3rd Regiment Army Air Corps (Lynx and Gazelle attack helicopters)
- 13 Air Assault Support Regiment
- 156 Provost Company, Royal Military Police

And, of course, on the most special operations assets brought into the ITO by the United Kingdom were the operators from 22 SAS.

Britain's generals entrusted with leading the large contingent into battle represented a new generation of military commander whose operational experience touched upon the scorched earth of the Balkans, Africa, and Afghanistan (with tours of service in Northern Ireland tossed in for good measure). The overall British commander was Air Marshal Brian Burridge, a veteran Nimrod pilot and staff officer; his chief of staff,

Major-General Barney White-Spunner, led the 16 Air Assault Brigade in Afghanistan. The Maritime Component Commander, Major-General Tony Milton was a veteran Royal Marines officer with years of service in Northern Ireland and Cyprus, while Land Component Commander Major-General Peter Wall, an experienced engineering and para officer, had led forces in Bosnia; air operations were commanded by Air Vice-Marshal Glenn Torpy, a Jaguar reconnaissance pilot, who served as assistant chief of staff for Operation *Desert Fox* in December 1998.

For British forces in the ITO, the conflict commenced weeks before the initial U.S. bombing of Baghdad on the night of March 19, 2003—operators from 22 SAS and the SBS were believed to have been operating *for weeks* inside Iraq gathering intelligence and executing direct action and sabotage strikes against key Iraqi military and political targets. But for the brunt of the British forces poised for the push into Iraq from bases in Kuwait, the primary push commenced on the night of March 20-21, when 3 Commando Brigade conducted an amphibious assault on the Al Faw

Soldiers from the 1st Battalion Royal Regiment of Fusiliers are given the order to move out against an Iraqi stronghold. (Courtesy: UK MoD)

Infantrymen from the 1st Battalion Royal Regiment of Fusiliers cover armored vehicles moving through a breach in the Iraqi field defenses. (Courtesy: UK MoD)

Airborne soldiers from 3 Para secure a minor pipeline. (Courtesy: UK MoD)

British vehicles move across the desert passing an oil well head had been set alight. The coalition advance was so fast and furious that much of the oil infrastructure in southern Iraq was captured intact. (Courtesy: UK MoD)

peninsula, encountering light resistance. The British-led assault along the eastern and ultra-strategic Iraqi ports were a crucial element of the Allied war plans—seizing the Iraqi ports would allow for the massive supply effort to commence; seizing the refineries in and around Basra before Saddam Hussein's Republican Guards, Special Republican Guards and Fedayeen Saddam forces could destroy them in a scorched earth policy was crucial in maintaining the economic integrity of Iraq (there was great fear among Allied commanders that the Iraqis would unleash a flow of oil into the Persian Gulf in an act of desperate environmental terrorism). Along with the 3 Commando Brigade's amphibious operations, operators from the SBS along with a team from GROM, the Polish Army's counterterrorist and special operations force that spearheaded Poland's participation in "Operation Iraqi Freedom," secured oil rigs in the water, and safeguarded many of the approaches to Basra.

Along with the 3 Commando effort, elements of 1st (UK) Armoured Division punched a hole into Iraq along with other Allied coalition forces, thrusting towards Basra. U.S. Marines seized the port of Umm Qasr and Royal Navy mine-hunters began work to clear the associated waterways of any mines that the Iraqi Navy or other forces might have left behind as a parting gift. During the first day of the ground fighting, British air and naval assets were instrumental in providing both American and British ground forces with ample support—Tomahawk cruise missiles fired from Royal Navy submarines hit key command and control centers throughout the country (from Basra to Baghdad) and Royal Navy vessels provided close gun support to Royal Marines pushing in on the city. RAF Tornado GR4s and Harrier GR7s flew hundreds of close-support sorties over British forces, peppering Iraqi forces entrenched around Basra with an incessant shower of ordnance from the sky. The RAF also deployed its new Storm Shadow ASM for the first time against targets inside Baghdad and Basra.

From the onset, it was clear to British commanders on the ground that the fighting for Basra would not be a cakewalk. Although elements of the conventional Iraqi military, such as the Iraqi 51st Mechanized Division that surrendered to U.S. Marines and the British 7th Armoured Division, rather than face certain destruction, Saddam Hussein loyalists were determined to put up a fight to the death. The Iraqi tactic was classic guerrilla—hit-and-run warfare punctuated by hiding behind the human shield of the residents of the besieged city who were yearning from liberation. The Republic Guards, the fanatical Special Republic Guards, and the thug-like Fedayeen Saddam shed their camouflage and black fatigues to dress like everyday Iraqis. They blended in with the civilian population and attacked advancing British units with hit-and-run attacks, launching RPGs at advancing armor and vehicles, and sniping at British forces on patrol.

Between March 23 and March 26, British forces, including Royal Marines and mechanized infantrymen from the Black Watch found themselves engulfed in a wicked cat-and-mouse game of ballistic hit-and-be-hit; several British armored fighting vehicles were hit in ambushes and others were hit in friendly-fire incidents during the close-quarter conflagrations. The fighting was slow, arduous, bloody, and not the kind of fast moving modern mechanized war Britain's elite combat formations had come to fight. British forces began taking casualties—wounded, and killed in action. By March 24, Basra airport had been seized and secured by Challenger 2 MBTs. On March 25, in one of the largest conventional battles of the campaign for Basra, British forces completed operations to secure Umm Qasr while 3 Commando Brigade, supported by helicopters and U.S. and British aircraft, defeated an armored counterattack, destroying nineteen T-55 MBTs; British artillery destroyed Iraqi mortars and guns that had opened fire on Iraqi civilian areas in Basra. The next day, a combined force of British Marines, infantrymen and armor units

Marines from 42 Commando deploy from a 845 Squadron Sea King chopper during mopping up operations on the Al Faw peninsula. (Courtesy: UK MoD)

Marines from 42 Commando advance cautiously on the Al Faw peninsula. (Courtesy: UK MoD)

40 Commando on the Al Faw peninsula deploy against Iraqi positions. (Courtesy: UK MoD)

conducted raids against irregular forces in the Basra area; the Ba'ath Party headquarters in as-Samawah, a nearby provincial town, was destroyed. Iraqi tanks advancing out of Basra were engaged and destroyed. The next day, a squadron of the Royal Scots Dragoon Guards eliminated an Iraqi tank unit and infantry positions near Basra without suffering any losses.

When confronting conventional Iraqi military units, the British were able to slice through enemy lines with little difficulty. Iraqi armor and infantry units, softened by massive aerial bombardment and the victim of unopposed coalition aerial close air-to-ground support, were unable to mount any series coordinated resistance; Iraqi military commanders, poorly-trained and motivated by their own survival rather than the defense of the regime, were quick to surrender. The irregular forces who managed to take control of Basra, though, were fighting for their very lives—in a new Iraq, one where political accounts would be settled against those who perpetrated terror in the name of Saddam Hussein, those in the Republic Guards, the Special Republic Guards and the Fedayeen Saddam would be held accountable and Iraq being held accountable by those

Royal Marines from 42 Commando secure the area around Umm Qasr. (Courtesy: UK MoD)

A Royal Marine from 45 Commando stands guard in Umm Qasr during a pause in the action. (Courtesy: UK MoD)

A Royal Marine of 539 Assault Squadron during the mop up operations to secure Umm Qasr. (Courtesy: UK MoD)

seeking justice meant a firing squad…or worse! As a result, British forces entrusted with clearing the Basra corridor were tasked with a difficult mission—they had to conquer, safeguard and garrison Iraq's second-largest city *before* much of the Allied coalition effort reached Baghdad and Iraqi opposition officially collapsed.

On March 28 the true British push on Basra commenced. British forces moved to interdict northern routes into Basra, securing the major oil refinery at Basra and ensuring the integrity of the petroleum industry in the embattled country. The next day, 3 Commando Brigade launched an offensive near Basra and secured Abu al Khasib, a major transportation hub. On April 1, British troops destroyed Iraqi artillery and missiles near Basra and on April 3, British forces continued operations against paramilitary forces in and around Basra, and captured a ballistic missile battery near Az Zubayr. The fighting, for British forces, was neighborhood-to-neighborhood, street-to-street, house-to-house, and even room-to-room. The British military experience in Northern Ireland—as well as in Bosnia—was invaluable in the war-ravaged city. Soldier safety was an absolute concern to field commanders who had to make sure that operations against the Saddam Hussein loyalists did not harm the citizens of the city—many of whom were killed by Iraqi irregulars when they tried to leave the city and enter the safety of coalition-controlled zones.

On April 4, British forces expanded the area of control northwards from the main southern oilfields near Basra. By April 6, British forces established control over a large part of the city of Basra, with the 3rd Battalion The Parachute Regiment, clearing on foot the old quarter, inaccessible to vehicles. The *suq*, the ancient marketplace of the city, was a hornet's nest of Saddam Fedayeen activity; Iraqi snipers ringed rooftops and demolition charges were placed in choke points in and around the narrow alleyways of the old town. The Paras, though, were undeterred by the resistance. Organized in small-unit raiding parties, the Paras went into

A foot patrol from the Black Watch enters Al Zubayr. (Courtesy: UK MoD)

An armed Land Rover of 1 Para relieves a Scimitar of the Household Cavalry Regiment on reconnaissance patrol in southern Iraq. (Courtesy: UK MoD)

heading toward the tribal home towns and hoping that they could evade coalition road blocks and identity checks.

By April 10, elements of 1st (UK) Armoured Division pushed north from Basra towards the U.S.-held positions around al-Amarah, linking up the strategic axis control points of the coalition offensive and all-but sealing the fate of the rear areas still not under American or British control. By April 13, with much of Baghdad already under American-control and the Iraqi opposition all but vanished, Britain's forces in "Operation Telic" went from an offensive military force to one resigned to nation-building and day-to-day policing. In Basra, local police patrols were resumed under the close supervision of British troops. Much of the looting that erupted throughout Iraq—

A Scots crew with The Welsh Cavalry makes sure that there is no doubt about their nationality showing the flag in a proud and resolute manner. (Courtesy: UK MoD)

action clearing section by section of the old city; the fighting, for much of the two-days, was hand-to-hand and close-quarter. Two British soldiers were killed in operations and several seriously wounded, but the British advance through the city was undeterred. The next day British forces swept through the city eliminating the last remnants of Iraqi opposition. The Iraqi special operations units who had sworn to protect the city from the coalition juggernaut to the death and were still alive after the British push, escape proved to be the sole salvation from the city. These units crumbled once completely destroyed and they filtered out of the city,

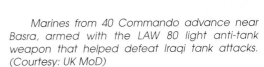

Marines from 40 Commando advance near Basra, armed with the LAW 80 light anti-tank weapon that helped defeat Iraqi tank attacks. (Courtesy: UK MoD)

especially in Baghdad—did not take place in Basra. British forces assumed a lock-down approach to law and order in the areas under their control. They also went to great lengths to ensure that the populations under their zones of influence had water and food.

Britain's contribution to "Operation Iraqi Freedom" was an instrumental element to the sweeping coalition victory. At the time of this article's writing thirty-two British servicemen were killed in the war again Saddam Hussein, and several hundred wounded. By mid-May 2003, much of Britain's contribution to the war effort was withdrawn; other units, such as the special operations units that punched a hole for the rest of the formations to push through, returned to the anonymous battlefield of the war against terrorism for missions in Afghanistan and elsewhere.

Marines from 42 Commando fight against a sand storm as they attempt to maintain their timetable during the push toward Basra. (Courtesy: UK MoD)

3 Commando Brigade Land Rovers pass a recently destroyed Iraqi T-55 MBT in the suburbs of Abu al-Khasib. (Courtesy: UK MoD)

Royal Marines of 40 Commando keep watch near Basra as civilians pass by in safety, wary of the ordnance coming in from the south and Saddam Fedayeen ordnance being lobbed from inside the city. (Courtesy: UK MoD)

An AS90 of 3rd Regiment Royal Horse Artillery provides artillery support to troops engaged in Basra. (Courtesy: UK MoD)

A Queen's Dragoon Guards Scimitar in the desert near Basra. (Courtesy: UK MoD)

A sniper from the RAF Regiment aims at a target from the top of his Land Rover. (Courtesy: UK MoD)

A Fusilier machine-gunner keeps watch as night falls over Basra. (Courtesy: UK MoD)

Vehicles of 40 Commando move ahead on the war-torn path toward the entrance to Basra. (Courtesy: UK MoD)

Royal Marines and US Marines on a joint patrol near Basra—as allies go, the British and American operational alliance was superb. (Courtesy: UK MoD)

The crew of an Irish Guards Warrior AIFV enjoys a brief rest near Basra—respites in the fighting were few and far between in the British sector. (Courtesy: UK MoD)

Liberated Iraqis reassure a Royal Marine of their allegiance and their fear of Saddam Hussein loyalists. (Courtesy: UK MoD)

A truck-load of the Royal Irish Guards moves up to help secure the oil fields near Basra. (Courtesy: UK MoD)

The Royal Regiment of Fusiliers battle group advances through southern Iraq on their way to Basra. (Courtesy: UK MoD)

A Warrior armored vehicle is guided over a bridge built by the Royal Engineers on the road to Basra. (Courtesy: UK MoD)

A Milan ATGW missile team of the Royal Regiment of Fusiliers search for a target at Basra—Milan batteries were extremely successful against Iraq's aging T-55s and building used by the Saddam Fedayeen as sniper positions. (Courtesy: UK MoD)

A Challenger 2 MBT of the Queen's Royal Lancers moves slowly on patrol near Basra. (Courtesy: UK MoD)

An Irish Guards sniper provides cover during an assault to clear pro-Saddam forces from a complex at Basra. (Courtesy: UK MoD)

The view from the top of an armed Land Rover used by sappers of 16 Air Assault Brigade for engineer reconnaissance. (Courtesy: UK MoD)

A Challenger 2 MBT of the Royal Scots Dragoon Guards, 7th Armoured Brigade, provides support to 3 Commando Brigade in southern Basra. (Courtesy: UK MoD)

The reconnaissance platoon Land Rovers of 1st Battalion, The Royal Irish Regiment, cross a canal with the help of M3 ferry (Courtesy: UK MoD)

A Royal Marines patrol alongside one of the waterways leading toward the northern approaches of Basra. (Courtesy: UK MoD)

Soldiers from 3 Para on patrol on the streets of Basra. (Courtesy: UK MoD)

A Challenger 2 MBT from the Queen's Royal Lancers on guard duty in Basra. (Courtesy: UK MoD)

A soldier of the Royal Regiment of Fusiliers guards a Styx anti-ship missile found in the Maqal area of Basra. (Courtesy: UK MoD)

Royal Marines enter a building during a search operation in downtown Basra. Because of the Royal Marines' vast experiences in house-to-house counterinsurgency operations in Northern Ireland, the "green berets" were ideally suited for ops in Basra. (Courtesy: UK MoD)

Hovercraft are in use with 3 Commando Brigade for patrols along Basra's waterways. (Courtesy: UK MoD)

"Operation Falconer"
The Australian Effort in Iraq

Australian CH-47s from the 5th Aviation Regiment over western Iraq drop flares before deploying with a mixed force of American and Australian special forces. (Australian MoD)

Operators from the 4th Battalion, Royal Australian Regiment (Commando) patrol and clear buildings and infrastructure in a major Iraqi airbase in western Iraq with the battered warplane in the background. (Australian MoD)

Like the United Kingdom, Australia has been a traditional ally of the United States ready, willing, and able to send its military forces to the world's hotspots in the struggle against international aggression and terrorism. Australia was one of the first and most outspoken supporters of America's war against terrorism, deploying Australian special operations units alongside America's counterterrorist forces in Afghanistan. When the United States sought international military support for the war against Saddam Hussein, Australia was, again, one of the first on board. Australia's contribution to the coalition, known as Operation Falconer, has to date involved about 2,000 Australian Defense Force personnel, and included:

- 250 airmen and women and support crews deployed with a squadron of 14 Royal Australian Air Force F/A-18 Hornet fighter aircraft.
- 150 personnel deployed with three RAAF C-130 Hercules transport aircraft.

- 150 personnel deployed with two P-3C Orion maritime patrol aircraft.
- An Air Forward Command Element of approximately seventy personnel responsible for coordinating air operations with coalition partners and providing national control of RAAF assets.
- Approximately 350 sailors and soldiers embarked on the sea transport ship HMAS *Kanimbla* with a Sea King helicopter, as well as army landing craft and army air defense detachments with a specialist explosives ordnance team.
- About 600 personnel embarked on Royal Australian Navy frigates HMA Ships *Anzac* and *Darwin*.
- A Navy clearance diving team capable of locating, rendering safe and disposing of mines.
- A Special Forces Task Group of about 500 personnel, including: (a) An advance party including a Special Air Service squadron. (b) CH-47 troop-lift helicopters and personnel from the 5th Aviation Regiment.

Commandos from the 4th Battalion, Royal Australian Regiment (Commando) patrol and clear buildings at a major Iraqi military installation in western Iraq. (Australian MoD)

(c) Specialist troops tasked to deal with the threat of weapons of mass destruction drawn from the Incident Response Regiment based at Holsworthy, New South Wales.
- A quick reaction support force drawn from the Holsworthy-based 4RAR Commando unit and a Combat Service Support Group that provides the essential logistic support necessary for all these elements to remain functional.
- An Australian National Headquarters of approximately sixty personnel, headed by the Australian National Commander, Brigadier-General Maurie McNarn.

Australian forces assigned to "Operation Iraqi Freedom" operated primarily in western Iraq, hunting possible SCUD launchers, searching for bases that shielded weapons of mass destruction, and cutting off escape routes of Saddam Hussein loyalists into Syria and Jordan. On April 11, Australian forces commenced "Operation Baghdad Assist," to help deliver medical supplies to the city.

Australian SAS operators deploy in ambush formation in the darkened Iraqi desert near the border with Jordan. (Australian MoD)

Australian SAS operators conduct a night patrol on a remote range at night. (Australian MoD)

Australian soldiers from the 4th Battalion, Royal Australian Regiment check captured ammunition from a Republic Guard base in western Iraq near the Jordanian frontier. (Australian MoD)

A 4th Battalion, Royal Australian Regiment (Commando) operator negotiates the harsh reality of an Iraqi desert sandstorm during a search-and-destroy operation for Saddam Hussein's weapons of mass destruction. (Australian MoD)

Sergeant Charlie Kearnan, from the Royal Australian Air Force Airfield Defense Guard detachment, patrols the Australian section of Baghdad International Airport air traffic control tower. The controllers and RAAF support staff are protected in their location by a detachment of Airfield Defense Guards. The detachment conducts regular foot patrols around the Australian section of the airport, ensuring a precise knowledge of the ground and potential threats in the area. (Australian MoD)

A 5th Aviation Regiment air crew maintains a tactical watch over a flight of CH-47s heading for an operation near the Jordanian border. (Australian MoD)

"LIGHTNING STORM II"

Evacuation Training for 3-158 Aviation Regiment
Carl Schulze

21 August 2002, 1246 hours: First in, last out. The scouts of HHC, 1-63 Armor are extracted after having protected the extraction of all other assets involved in the NEO. Speed is a critical factor in this part of the operation since cover is only provided by the AH-64A Apache, and helicopters and troops in the PZ are vulnerable targets for enemy attack or sniper fire.

With the end of the Cold War, civil wars or wars between small countries became a common reality, especially in Africa, the Middle East and Asia. Quite often civilians such as tourists, employees of humanitarian help organizations and business travelers from foreign countries have become trapped in such conflicts. This situation has often forced western nations to take action to rescue their citizens using their armed forces. Examples of rescue operations in recent years are the evacuation of civilians from the Congo by troops of the French Foreign Legion in 1997,

20 August 2002, 1700 hours. As part of the planning of the operation, all pilots and key players of the NEO from all involved units are briefed and take part in a dry run of the operation conducted on a model of the operational area. During the dry run, all necessary procedures are rehearsed in detail, including flight routes, landing zones, radio frequencies, alternative landing zones, FARP procedures, timings, and so on. What may look like a relaxed discussion is in fact highly concentrated work to discover weak points or overlooked details that could cause the operation to fail.

20 August 2002, 1815. In the TOC of the 3-158 AVN, the latest tactical information is marked on the map. Since the establishment of the TOC at Giebelstadt US Army Airfield on 19 August, the HQ staff was kept busy planning every detail of the coming NEO. They covered details such as take-off and landing times, establishing FARPs, flight routes, communications, etc.

21 August 2002, 1045 hours. Outside the US embassy, protestors demonstrate against the presence of US citizens in Bonnland. Occasionally, the embassy was attacked by small arms fire from the surrounding tree line. Later the protesters began to throw sticks and stones and tried to enter the embassy. But the arrival of the first US troops on the ground deterred them and sent the protesters running. Note that even the protesters were equipped with MILES equipment to simulate the effect of weapons fire.

21 August 2002, 1115 hours. One of the four AH-64A Apache combat helicopters of A Troop, 2nd Sqn, 6th Cavalry checks LZ/PZ "Sparrow" for enemy activity. It was the AH-64A Apache pilots who discovered that LZ "Eagle" was unsuitable due to enemy activity and that LZ/PZ "Sparrow" had to be used as an alternative. For reconnaissance, the crew of the aircraft uses the nose-mounted TADS (Target Acquisition and Designation Sight). The TADS comprises a FLIR (Forward Looking Infrared), a TV camera, a laser tracker, and a laser range finder/designator. For night operations, the AH-64A Apache helicopter is fitted with the PNVS (Pilot Night Vision Sensor). Mounted under the nose of the AH-64A is the M230A-1 30mm Chain Gun that has a rate of fire of 625 rounds per minute. The stub wings on the sides each have two pylons under which AGM 114 Hellfire and pods with nineteen 2.75in Hydra 70 FFAR rockets can be mounted. This Apache is fitted with the Hydra rocket pods and a MILES system for simulation of the Hellfire missile.

the extraction of European citizens from Rwanda by Belgian Para Commandos in 1994, and the German operation "Libelle", during which civilians were extracted from Albania in 1997.

US forces also conducted an evacuation of civilians from the unstable Albania in 1997 in an operation called "Silver Wake". Other recent US

21 August 2002, 1131 hours: H-Hour. The first wave of four UH-60Ls of the 3-158 AVN takes off from LZ/PZ "Sparrow" after inserting the 44-soldier security force. During takeoff, the helicopter crew members use 7.62mm M60 machine guns mounted in the aircraft's side doors to provide cover fire for the troops exposed in the landing zone.

21 August 2002, 1132 hours. The second wave of UH-60L Black Hawks has reached LZ/PZ "Sparrow" and is dropping off its load of 24 US Marines. At the same time, the soldiers of the US Army were already involved in heavy fighting with the militia. However, this battle drew the attention of the militia away from the incoming second wave of transport helicopters.

operations conducted with the aim of rescuing civilians from a war-shaken country were Operation "Eastern Exit" in Somalia in 1991, Operation "Distant Runner" in Rwanda in 1994, Operation "Noble Obelisk" in Sierra Leone in 1997, and an operation in Eritrea in 2000. Sometimes the evacuation of civilians formed part of larger combat operations. For example, in the 1983 US Grenada campaign, troops evacuated over 1000 US citizens. In the modern US military vocabulary, such an operation is known as a Non-combatant Evacuation Operation or NEO.

What is a NEO?

In the US Field Manual FM 1-100 Army Aviation Operations, the Non-combatant Evacuation Operation is described as follows:

"NEO relocate threatened civilian non-combatants from locations in a foreign country or host nation. These operations may involve US citizens

A crewmember of a UH-60L Black Hawk of 3-158 AVN observes LZ/PZ "Sparrow" while the aircraft touches down. He has his hands on one of the 7.62mm M60 machine guns that were mounted in the helicopters for self-defense and fire support purposes.

21 August 2002, 1135 hours. Scouts of HHC, 1-63 Armor use their 7.62mm M240B machine gun to suppress troops of a local militia. Securing the box perimeter around LZ "Sparrow" was hard work and the rescue force took several casualties. Behind the machine gunner, a group of his comrades are ready to attack the position once the enemy has moved under cover.

21 August 2002, 1136 hours. Playing the role of irregular forces, troops of the British 16th Signal Regiment engage the scouts of 1-63 Armor who have just landed. The fire of the British troops provided a hot welcome for the US troops in LZ/PZ "Sparrow". In addition to their well-prepared positions, the British soldiers barricaded all approaches to their positions in order to slow down the advance of the US soldiers and give them a hard time before they could report that the PZ was safe.

a joint-US-force training exercise for such a NEO and all of its critical situations, including the loss of a UH-60L Black Hawk through hostile fire. Participating in the exercise were troops from the US Army, US Air Force and the United States Marine Corps.

21 August 2002, 1136 hours. A scout of HHC, 1-63 Armor engages enemy positions while securing a box perimeter around LZ/PZ "Sparrow". The soldier is armed with a 5.56mm M4A1 KAC carbine fitted with a forward handgrip and a reflex sight.

whose lives are in danger; they may include selected host nation citizens or third country nationals. NEO may be conducted in the environments of conflict or war in a peaceful, orderly fashion or may require forcible means. Aviation forces are employed in the rapid air movement of non-combatants from endangered areas not safely served by fixed-wing aircraft. Scout and attack aircraft provide security for the air movement; they are prepared to engage hostile elements that may attempt to interfere with NEO".

A NEO is a difficult operation in which armed forces often operate in an area where the status of hostile forces is unclear and the rules of engagement are complicated. Therefore, the force might easily become involved in the fighting between different warring factions such as local militias and the host nation's armed forces. Another problem might be the gathering of, identification of, and co-operation with the civilians who have to be extracted.

Command and control can also create a critical issue since the extraction force most likely will have to operate remotely, far away from its operational base but react quickly to a changing situation. The operation could become even more complicated due to its joint character involving troops from various services such as the Army, Air Force, Marines, and Navy. Lack of intelligence about the operational area and potential enemy forces often provides additional problems. In August 2002, Bonnland, Germany's prime training site for fighting in built-up areas, was the site of

The soldiers of the British 16th Signal Regiment prepared sections of Bonnland, the German FIBUA village, to look as realistic as possible. This building clearly illustrates that Americans are not welcome in Bonnland. Note the .50 M2 HB machine gun that gave the US NEO Task Force a hard time when they landed.

21 August 2002, 1230 hours. Guided by US Marines, the 36 US citizens are evacuated by CH-47D transport helicopters of F Company, 159th Aviation. Prior to the evacuation, the civilians were searched for weapons and explosives, their identities were checked, and a medic checked their health status. To make training more realistic, most of the civilians were carrying some personal belongings; one even brought along his dog and another pretended to resist evacuation.

21 August 2002, 1231 hours. A US Marine from the US Marine Security Force Company – Island (foreground) provides cover with his 5.56mm M16A2 with a 40mm M203 grenade launcher mounted underneath. In the background, the civilian who resisted evacuation is taken on board the CH-47D of F Company, 159th Aviation Regiment.

Exercise Scenario for "Lightning Storm II"

Exercise "Lightning Storm II" took place between 19 and 21 August 2002. The training objectives for the exercise were the following:

- Task force air assault and conduct of an NEO.
- Exercise command and control of the task force during the whole operation with changing situations and orders using radio retransmission sites
- Using an air and ground TAC.
- CSAR (Combat Search and Rescue).
- Establish and maintain two FARPs (Forward Arming and Refueling Point) using CH-47D Fat Cow and M978 HEMTT tankers.
- Train joint combined arms operations.

In the scenario of the exercise, a group of 36 American civilians was trapped in the US embassy of the fictitious state of Bonnland. The nation's government had collapsed, militias were now ruling, and US civilians and US establishments had become targets for anti-American protesters. Anti-American

21 August 2002, 1138 hours. After being flown into LZ/PZ "Sparrow", US Marines assemble close to the LZ before moving out to secure the US Embassy. The Marine in the foreground is armed with a 5.56mm M249 SAW. Note that most of these elite American soldiers wear protective goggles to shield their eyes from sand and small stones that could easily be thrown up by the down wash of the rotor blades.

21 August 2002, 1232 hours. A machine-gun team from the scouts platoon, HHC, 1-63 Armor observes the surrounding of PZ "Sparrow" while CH-47D Chinook transport helicopters evacuate US citizens. The team is armed with the 7.62mm M240B machine gun and wears MILES equipment for simulating combat situations.

21 August 2002, 1233 hours. While the CH-47Ds of F Company, 159th AVN "Big Windy" evacuate the civilians, scouts from HHC, 1-63 Armor guard the pick-up zone against attacks from the local militias. The soldier in the rear is equipped with a 7.62mm M240B machine gun, while the soldier in the foreground is armed with a 5.56mm M4A1 KAC carbine fitted with forward handgrip. For realistic duel and casualty simulation, all troops taking part in the NEO, as well as the hostile forces, were equipped with MILES.

demonstrations were conducted outside the US embassy and the lives of US civilians were threatened. The US governor, therefore, had gathered the Americans living in the country into his embassy, and the US Government decided to conduct a NEO in order to transport the civilians to safety.

The first combat troops to be deployed into Bonnland were soldiers of a long range surveillance detachment from 165th Military Intelligence Battalion, E Company, 51st Infantry. The soldiers deployed on 19 August at 2230 hours. Their mission was to provide the TOC of the 3rd Battalion, 158th Aviation Regiment (which since 1745 hours on 19 August was situated in the FOB at Giebelstadt) with first hand information on the situation on the ground. In addition, the troops linked up with the US embassy and looked for suitable helicopter landing sites. Among other information, the intelligence soldiers provided information on the strength and equipment of the local militias, as well as their positions and activities.

It became clear that soldiers of the UF and OF were operating in the area of the planned NEO in nearly equal strength, numbering 30 to 40 men, and opposing each other. Both sides were committing murder and arson, rioting, bombing, looting, and carrying out drive-by shootings. In addition, a group of 50 armed anti-American activists were spreading propaganda

21 August 2002, 1243 hours. The US Marines from the US Marine Security Force Company – Island usually guard the US Embassy in Keflavik. During Exercise "Lightning Storm II", their mission was to evacuate the US citizens safely from the Bonnland embassy. Following the successful departure of the civilians, a Marine armed with a 9mm Beretta 92FS pistol (called the M9 by the US forces) takes cover in a wooded area close to the PZ while he awaits his own extraction.

21 August 2002, 1243 hours. Following the successful evacuation of the civilians from Bonnland, a Marine with a fiercely camouflaged face takes up a position in the woods close to the PZ prior to his own pick-up.

21 August 2002, 1138 hours. After being flown into LZ/PZ "Sparrow", US Marines gather near the LZ before they move out to secure the US Embassy. The weaponry of the Marine four-man fire team consists of one 5.56mm M16A2 fitted with a 40mm M203 grenade launcher, one 5.56mm M249 SAW light machine gun and two 5.56mm M16A2 assault rifles. Note that most of the Marines wear wind-, sand- and dust-protection goggles.

and demonstrating outside the embassy. All three groups were armed with automatic rifles, machine guns, light anti-tank weapons, and shoulder-launched air defense weapons.

Insertion of the Security Force

After intensive planning and rehearsal, the task force consisting of troops of the US Army, US Marine Corps and US Air Force began the NEO on the morning of 21 August 2002. At 1000 hours the AH-64A Apache combat helicopters were the first aircraft to take off from the operational base at Giebelstadt US Army Air Base. They were followed at 1030 hours by four UH-60L Black Hawk helicopters carrying the security force provided by troops of HHC, 1st Battalion, 63rd Armor Regiment. At 1032 the second batch of four UH-60L Black Hawks carrying the USMC evacuation party took off. In order to provide the troops with some challenges, exercise control placed enemy troops in LZ "Eagle", the planned landing zone for the security force. The enemy was discovered,

though, and from his TAC the commander of the task force re-directed the helicopters already approaching Bonnland to the alternate landing zone, LZ "Sparrow".

During this phase of the exercise it became obvious that communication between all assets involved in a NEO is vital to the success of the operation. During Exercise "Lightning Storm II", all types of communication were used, including UHF, VHF, FM and HF radios, as well as SATCOM. To extend the range of some of the systems involved, retransmission stations provided by 17th Signal Battalion of V (US) Corps were established.

21 August 2002, 1246 hours. The cover force from HHC, 1-63 Armor has safely boarded the UH-60L helicopters of 3-158 AVN. The UH-60L can carry up to 11 combat loaded troops or an underslung Royal Ordnance 105mm Light Gun and 30 rounds of ammunition. Note how the troops point their weapons to the aircraft floor, a common procedure that is followed to prevent damage to vital parts of the helicopter like the engine or rotor in case a weapon is accidentally fired.

21 August 2002, 1247 hours. While the troops of the assault force return to the helicopters that will extract them to safety after a successful mission, the AH-64A Apache combat helicopters of A Troop, 2nd Sqn, 6th Cavalry cover the extraction.

21 August 2002, 1247 hours. Although the first helicopter had been shot down, the three remaining helicopters take off from PZ "Sparrow" to extract the cover force. The decision to leave behind the wreck and possible survivors was made to prevent the loss of more aircraft and personnel in an uncoordinated ad-hoc rescue conducted by the security force. A CSAR force was kept on hand especially for such a scenario.

The first wave to touch down in alternate landing zone "Sparrow" near the US embassy consisted of 4 UH-60L Black Hawks carrying 44 soldiers of the scout platoon and the mortar platoon of the 1st Battalion, 63rd Armor Regiment. As soon as the helicopters touched down, local militias portrayed by British soldiers of the 16th Signal Regiment began to engage the enemy with small arms fire. The US Army soldiers' mission was to secure a box perimeter around the helicopter landing site (HLS) in order to allow a safe delivery of the extraction forces and, later, the planned evacuation of the civilians. After the US troops spread out from the airframes, they immediately began to close in on the enemy positions. While the US Army troops were still fighting with the militia forces in order to secure the LZ/PZ, the second wave of four UH-60L Black Hawks touched down and delivered the 24-man evacuation force from the US Marine Corps Security Force Company based in Island. After the

helicopters had left, the Marines assembled near the LZ and moved out to the nearby US Embassy.

Rescue and Extraction of the Non-Combatants

The appearance of the heavily armed US Marines at the embassy site deterred the anti-American protesters and they soon disappeared. On their arrival at the embassy, part of the small force set up a security perimeter around the embassy while the remaining marines started to prepare the evacuation of the non-combatants. ID cards were checked, personal belongings were searched for weapons and explosives, the health of the

A UH-60L Black Hawk of the 3-158 AVN touches down at LZ "Sparrow". The UH-60L Black Hawk is the US Army's front line utility helicopter. The US Army fielded the first version of the Black Hawk, the UH-60A, in 1978. In 1989, the UH-60A was replaced by the UH-60L, which has 24 percent more power thanks to an improved engine and power train. The UH-60L seen here is fitted with the External Stores Support System (ESSS), which allows sixteen Hellfire missiles or other weapon systems to be carried. Alternatively, external fuel tanks can be mounted to the ESSS, extending the range of the UH-60L to 1150 nautical miles. This UH-60L is fitted with fuel tanks.

21 August 2002, 1305 hours. One of the two UH-60L Black Hawks from 3-158 AVN that make up the CSAR force inserts the rescue team. The helicopter is fitted with the External Stores Support System (ESSS) that allows the aircraft to carry two external fuel tanks, thereby extending the range of the UH-60L to 1150 nautical miles.

21 August 2002, 1315 hours. Soldiers belonging to the mortar platoon of HHC, 1-63 Armor close in on a hotel building during the rescue of the downed aircraft crew who took shelter there. All soldiers are armed with the M4A1 KAC carbine, which is the perfect sized weapon for operations in built-up areas and for troops travelling in helicopters. Three of the four weapons are fitted with reflex scopes while the fourth has a M203 grenade launcher mounted under the barrel.

21 August 2002, 1319 hours. A member of the CSAR team belonging to HHC, 1-63 Armor awaits the arrival of the extraction helicopters. The bright red panel he holds serves to signal the pilots of the position of the team on the ground. The Ranger badge worn above the 1st Infantry Division "The Big Red One" shoulder patch identifies him as one of the finest soldiers in the US Army.

21 August 2002, 1316 hours. Soldiers from the mortar platoon of HHC, 1-63 Armor take up a position near the hotel where the crew of the downed aircraft took shelter. The soldier in front is armed with an M4 carbine. Note the M203 grenade launcher mounted under the barrel.

Forward Arming and Refueling Points

"Lightning Storm II" also served as training in the use of Forward Arming and Refueling Points (FARP). A FARP is a fuel station for helicopters established in the operational area of the aircraft in order to extend operational time and range. During Exercise "Lightning Storm II", this was done by one FARP using two M978 HEMTT tankers each holding 9463 liters (2500 gallons) of aircraft fuel. During the NEO, FARP "Chevy" was used to refuel the eight UH-60L Black Hawk helicopters that inserted the security forces prior to returning to Bonnland to extract the security force after their operation was completed. FARP "Chevy" had the capability to refuel all eight aircraft at the same time. The second FARP, which was called "Corvette", consisted of a CH-47D Fat Cow that was used to refuel the AH-64A Apache combat helicopters. The Extended Range Fuel System (ERFS) II system is located in the cargo bay inside a CH-47D Fat Cow. The configuration consists of three or four fuel tanks containing up to 9084 liters (2400 gallons) of fuel attached to a refueling system with up to four refueling points.

Black Hawk Down in Bonnland

Everything went well up to 1245 hours when the last four UH-60Ls went in to pick up the soldiers of the 1st Battalion, 63rd Armor Regiment who had provided safety for the LZ. While the helicopters took off crammed with GIs, exercise control decided that one was hit by fire from the enemy and crashed into the LZ. All the infantrymen on board were killed during the crash and only two of the three crewmembers survived. The downed aircrew members ran from the crash site to safety, hiding themselves in a Bonnland hotel building that scouts had cleared of enemy troops earlier that same day.

civilians was checked, and the people were briefed on the upcoming extraction. Once these procedures were finished the Marines called in the CH-47Ds to pick up the civilians. In the meantime, the army units managed to secure the PZ and push back the hostile militia.

While the CH-47D Chinook of F Company, 159th Aviation Regiment landed, the US Marines guided the non-combatants from the embassy building to the HLS. During this march, the Marines tried to form a close shield of bodies around the civilians and pointed their weapons outward in the direction of possible danger. To make training more realistic, most of the 36 civilians were carrying some personal belongings; one even brought along his dog, and another pretended to resist the evacuation. After the CH-47D Chinook had left the PZ, the Marines assembled in a wooded area near the PZ and prepared themselves to be evacuated by four UH-60L Black Hawks that appeared seconds later.

21 August 2002, 1325 hours. UH-60L helicopters from 3-158 AVN take off from LZ/PZ "Sparrow" after the successful CSAR operation. The UH-60L Black Hawk was designed to operate in hot landing zones and, therefore, the protective armor of the helicopter can withstand hits from 23mm shells. The seats of the pilot and co-pilot are also armor-protected. However, despite these features three helicopters were lost to RPG fire in 1993 during an operation in Mogadishu, a case that vividly illustrates the vulnerability of helicopters operating over built-up areas.

were flown into LZ/PZ "Sparrow" and secured the area, then a four-man fire team closed in on the position where the downed aircrew had taken cover, linked up with them and escorted them out. Once contact was made, the rescue party and the two aircrew members returned to the PZ, where only seconds later they were picked up by helicopter and flown to safety.

The Mission of the AH-64A Apache during "Lightning Storm II"

Another vital part of the NEO Task Force that was involved in the exercise were four AH-64A Apache combat helicopters from A Troop, 2nd Squadron, 6th Cavalry Regiment, 11th Attack Helicopter Regiment. These combat helicopters conducted road and area reconnaissance prior to the transport helicopter carrying the assault force to Bonnland. It was the

21 August 2002, 1320 hours. After the CSAR team's successful rescue of the downed aircrew, a team member guides the two UH-60Ls of 3-158 AVN to the pick-up zone. At the same time, other team members provide security for the PZ. An A-10 Thunderbolt II of the US Air Force and an AH-64A Apache attack helicopter of 2nd Sqn, 6th Cavalry assist in this task.

Once under cover, the pilots activated their emergency radios on the pre-set rescue frequency and reported their position to the command helicopter still in the area. Of course, the other three crewmen of the remaining UH-60L Black Hawks had already reported the incident to the TAC. Here the battalion commander decided to call in support from the USAF in order to secure the crash site against further attacks by enemy forces. Within minutes four A-10 Thunderbolt II ground fighter aircraft of 81st Fighter Squadron, which had been kept ready for exactly this type of situation, began to patrol the airspace over Bonnland and provided close air support (CAS) by engaging a hostile force closing in on the crash site.

Along with calling out the fighter aircraft, the TAC ordered a CSAR operation (Combat Search and Rescue) to be conducted. The ensuing rescue mission was coordinated from the TAC, which from the beginning of the NEO was circling over Bonnland in a Command and Control (C_) UH-60A Black Hawk of A Company, 5th Battalion, 158th Aviation Regiment. Again troops of HHC, 1st Battalion, 63rd Armor Regiment

A profile shot of a pilot of a UH-60L from B Company, 3-158 AVN. The company is nicknamed "War Eagles".

Close-up of a UH-60L Black Hawk pilot of B Company, 3-158 AVN.

During Exercise "Lightning Storm II", the 5-58 AVN provided command and air traffic control assets. These assets were responsible for ensuring that peacetime air traffic regulations were met during the exercise. They were also tasked with coordinating the operational side of the air traffic. This photograph shows one of the unit's communication vehicles based on a HMMWV.

Apache crews who reported enemy activity in LZ "Eagle", which consequently led to the use of LZ "Sparrow".

During the approach to Bonnland, the combat helicopters searched the evacuation force's approach route for enemy air defense sites and eliminated them. Elements of 3rd Battalion, 4th Air Defense Artillery Regiment played the enemy. After the insertion of the first ground elements, the AH-64A pilots used the weapons on their helicopters to support the soldiers of the 1st Battalion, 63rd Armor Regiment in their mission to establish a box perimeter around the LS. Later, the Apaches aided in the safe evacuation of the American citizens and escorted the CH-47D out of the area. During the combat search-and-rescue operation, they again were deployed to assist with attack-by-fire to support the inserted

In an interview about Exercise "Lightning Storm II" following the NEO, a soldier from HHC, 1-63 Armor told a reporter of V Corps Public Affairs: "We had practiced bounding techniques, pulling security and moving through open areas, but I'm not sure we were prepared for that kind of assault." That fact is reflected in the face of this young GI who has just came under fire from the enemy militia.

rescue party. In this case, the combat helicopters co-operated closely with the A-10 Thunderbolt II of the US Air Force of the 81st Fighter Squadron and provided information on opposing forces and their movement on the ground.

The Helicopter: A Key Factor in a NEO

One of the key factors of a NEO is the ability to deploy a capable extraction force into the unstable country and extract it along with the rescued non-combatants. This can be done on the sea using landing crafts, on land by entering the country in vehicles from a friendly neighboring country, or by air using fixed wing aircraft or helicopters. In the past, the helicopter often was the most suitable way of insertion and extraction as these aircraft do not have the limitations of vehicles and fixed wing aircraft, and when refueled air-to-air or via a FARP, they can achieve nearly the same range. With helicopters, it is possible to conduct a NEO operation from multiple directions, which makes it hard for a hostile force to react. Using the latest night vision technology, such an operation can also be carried out under the cover of darkness and in nearly all weather conditions.

However, the use of helicopters also has limitations that can affect the planning and conduct of the actual NEO. Extreme environmental effects such as temperature and altitude can reduce the capabilities of the aircraft, especially its lift capacity, range and ceiling. During longer operations, helicopters require large amounts of fuel and spare parts, as well as extensive maintenance support. Also, terrain may limit the availability of adequate landing sites. Cargo helicopters such as the UH-60L Black Hawk have a large IR signature that makes them vulnerable to air defense missiles fitted with a heat-seeking warhead. In addition, NEOs, which usually take part in urban terrain, present unique and complex challenges to the helicopters and crews of aviation units. Restricted or limited landing zones (LZ) and pickup zones (PZ) might be lined with hazardous objects such as towers, antenna, and wires. Another potential problem is foreign object damage to the helicopters from debris raised by the down wash of the rotor blades. Also, hostile forces hiding inside the buildings surrounding the LZs and PZs and lining the approach and departure routes could use small arms at close range to create a high risk to the helicopters.

A situation that could add further complications during a NEO is the expected proximity of non-combatants and the danger they would face if the crew returned fire, which could produce collateral damage among uninvolved civilians and their property. Further, the use of night vision equipment in a built-up area can be hampered by the city's streetlights, and battlefield smoke and dust can obstruct vision and have a detrimental effect on helicopter operations. Last but not least, communication of all assets involved can be degraded during an operation in a built-up area due to the shielding effect of the buildings.

From Paper Play to Inter-Service-Level TrainingNEO training was introduced into the training schedule of the 3rd Battalion, 158th Aviation Regiment in 2001, well before the crisis of 11 September. Due to an official statement made before the terrorist attacks, the importance of NEO training was underestimated. But 2002 saw a change in the training policy,

and together with other units from V "Victory" Corps, the 3rd Battalion, 158th Aviation Regiment conducted several exercises focusing on NEO.

Today, NEO training is conducted regularly, not only with troops from 3rd Battalion, 158th Aviation Regiment but also with joint and combined forces. Of the exercises already conducted, "Lightning Storm 2002" is the latest highlight. What began as unit-level paper play by August 2002 had reached high standards and the inter-service level; it clearly demonstrates the ability of the US Army, US Air Force and US Marine Corps to look after US civilians trapped and threatened anywhere in the world.

Background on the US Army Corps Aviation Brigade

Each US Army corps has an aviation brigade among its organic assets. In the case of the Germany-based V (US) Corps, this is 12th Aviation Brigade. Although the aviation brigades differ slightly in size and construction among the various corps of the US Army, basically they consist of a headquarters and headquarters company (HHC), one aviation group and an attack regiment.

The aviation group normally consists of an aviation group HHC, an assault helicopter battalion (AHB), a command aviation battalion (CAB), a combat support aviation battalion (CSAB), a CH–47 helicopter battalion, a light utility helicopter (LUH) battalion, and an assigned ATS battalion. Due to the size of the of V Corps, which fields only two instead of the usual three combat divisions, 12th Aviation Brigade consists of the following units: Headquarters and Headquarters Company, 12th Aviation Brigade, 3rd Battalion, 158th Aviation Regiment (Assault Helicopter Battalion); 5th Battalion, 158th Aviation Regiment (Command Aviation Battalion); 3-58th Aviation Regiment (Air Traffic Services Battalion); and F Company, 159th Aviation Regiment (Heavy Lift Helicopter Company - attached to 3-158th Aviation Regiment).

Usually the attack regiment consists of a regimental HHC and three attack helicopter battalions. In the case of 12th Aviation Brigade, the attack regiment is 11th Aviation Regiment, which consists of HHC, 11th Aviation Regiment and two attack-helicopter units: 2nd Squadron, 6th Cavalry and 6th Squadron, 6th Cavalry. Both units are equipped with AH-64A Apaches and have currently started to receive the AH-64D Longbow Apache. The corps support command (COSCOM) provides an aviation maintenance battalion to support the aviation brigade; for V Corps in Germany this is 7th Battalion, 159th Aviation Maintenance Regiment.

The corps aviation brigade primarily conducts attack, reconnaissance, security, air assault, command and control (C^2), air movement operations, and air traffic service (ATS) throughout the area of operations (AO) of the corps. The corps aviation brigade plans, co-ordinates and executes aviation operations to support the scheme of maneuver of the corps. It can be expected to operate anywhere in the corps area. Attack helicopter units destroy enemy forces by fire and maneuver. Assault and transport helicopter units transport combat personnel, supplies, and equipment for corps operations. Helicopters are provided to corps units requiring heliborne C^2 assets. ATS are provided for Army airspace command and control integration, airspace information, and terminal and forward area

Badge of A Company, 5-158 AVN Regiment.

Badge of 12th Aviation Brigade and Headquarters and Headquarters Company, 12th Aviation Brigade.

Badge of 3-158 AVN Regiment.

The badge of 2nd Squadron, 6th Cavalry.

support services. Elements of the corps aviation brigade may operate directly for the corps commander or be placed under operational control of a subordinate division. The corps commander can task-organize other corps assets under the command of the corps aviation brigade or task the corps aviation brigade to support an armored cavalry unit. During operations, the aviation brigade in a corps without an armored cavalry regiment may be tasked with being the headquarters of the covering force, e.g., being responsible for the flanks during an attack. (After US Field Manual FM 1-100 Army Aviation Operations.)Units and Helicopters

Badge of A Company, 3-158 AVN Regiment.

Badge of F Company, 159th Aviation Regiment.

Badge of B Company, 3-158 AVN Regiment, nicknamed "War Eagles".

Participating in Exercise "Lightning Storm II"

12th Aviation Brigade
- 3rd Battalion, 158th Aviation Regiment
  * HHC
  * A Company (3x UH-60L Black Hawk)
  * B Company (7x UH-60L Black Hawk)
  * D Company
  * F Company, 159th Aviation Regiment (3x CH-47D Chinook)
- 5th Battalion, 158th Aviation Regiment
  * A Company (1x UH-60A Black Hawk)
- 5th Battalion, 58th Aviation Regiment (providing command and air traffic control assets)

11th Attack Helicopter Regiment
- 2nd Squadron, 6th Cavalry Regiment
  * A Troop (4x AH-64A Apache)

1st Infantry Division
- 3rd Battalion, 4th Air Defense Artillery Regiment (6x MANPAD Stinger, 2x Avenger)
- 1st Battalion, 63rd Armor Regiment
  * HHC (1x scout platoon, 1x mortar platoon)

205th Military Intelligence Brigade
- 165th Military Intelligence Battalion
  * E Company, 51st Infantry (Long Range Surveillance Detachment)

22nd Signal Brigade
- 17th Signal Battalion (1x retransmission vehicle)

United States Marine Corps
- US Marine Security Force Company - Island

United States Air Force
- 81st Fighter Squadron (4x A-10 Thunderbolt II)

OPFOR
- 16th Signal Regiment, Great Britain. Based at Brüggen in Germany.

Technical Data of the UH-60L Black Hawk

Crew:	3 (pilot, co-pilot and loadmaster)
Length:	64ft 10in
Height:	16ft 10in
Rotor diameter:	53ft 8in
Weight empty:	11,516lb
Mission gross weight:	17,432lb
Maximum gross weight:	22,000lb
Maximum gross weight (ferry):	24,500lb
Service ceiling ISA day:	19,150ft
Hover ceiling 95°F day:	7650ft
Hover ceiling standard day:	11,125ft
Vertical rate of climb at 4000ft 95F:	1550fpm
Vertical rate of climb at 2000ft 70F:	2750fpm
Maximum cruise speed 4000ft 95°f:	152kts
Maximum cruise speed 2000ft 70°f:	159kts
External lift capacity:	9000lb
Troop capacity:	11 fully equipped troops (Pax) or four stretchers in the MEDEVAC role
Engine:	2x General Electric T700-GE-700 Turboshaft Engines developing 1,940hp each
Armament:	2x M60D 7.62mm machine guns can be mounted optionally in the side doors with the M144 armament sub-system. With the M130 general purpose dispenser, chaff and infrared jamming flares can be used. When the External Stores Support System (ESSS) is used, sixteen Hellfire missiles or other weapon systems can be mounted externally. With the ESSS, external fuel tanks can also be mounted extending the range of the UH-60L to 1150 nautical miles.
Manufacturer:	United Technologies Sikorsky Aircraft, USA

New Challenges for
Operation "Unicorn"

Yves Debay

Seen here is another ERC-90 that destroyed both the Mercedes and the two 4x4 vehicles that were following it.

On 29 November 2002, a new rebel movement, the MPIGO (*Mouvement populaire ivoirien du Grand Ouest* – Popular Ivorian Movement of the Great West), captured the small city of Man in the western part of Ivory Coast. The capture of this city, along with the arrival of a third armed opposition movement, the MJP (*Mouvement pour la Justice et la Paix* – Movement for Justice and Peace), shook an Ivory Coast that was already well shaken by the failed coup of 19 September 2002 and the breakup of the country.

General Beth immediately engaged the CEA (*Compagnie d'élairage et d'appui* – Support and Recce Company) of the 2nd REP (Foreign Legion paratroops) and ERC-90 Sagaie armored cars of the 1st RIMa (Naval Infantry Regiment) – armored cars that are stockpiled in the 43rd BIMa (Naval Infantry Brigade) – in an operation to evacuate and protect western nationals. This is, after all, the primary mission of Operation Unicorn.

While reconnoitering the road that leads to the airport, two Sagaies and the REP's reconnaissance section become engaged with a strong rebel force supported by a mortar. RPG-7 rockets and bursts from Kalashnikovs

Elements of the 3rd Company of the 1st RCP man a French strongpoint at Tiébessous. In that sector, the soldiers of Operation Unicorn established the front line between the rebels of the MPCI and the FANCI. The bunker and sandbags is an obstacle that is very difficult for African soldiers to attack as they do not have the military sophistication to take such a position.

Three paratroopers of the 4th Company of the 1st RCP in a position in a bunker in the bush watch the road between Bouaké and Brobo. Note the various weapons: FAMAS, FR-F2 sniper rifle, and a Minimi light machine gun.

Soldiers of 4th Company, 1st RCP prepare to disembark from a Peugeot P-4 4x4 vehicle. To show that their mission is not military but supervisory, the paras wear berets and display a French flag on the vehicle.

shatter the serenity of an African sunset. The French soldiers reply and withdraw to a village where they remain on the defensive throughout the night. At dawn, the arrival of reinforcements and the heliborne delivery of a mortar and Milan section allow them to seize the airport. Ten rebels are killed and a Legionnaire is wounded. About 100 nationals are evacuated from the vicinity of Man, which the FANCI (*Forces armées nationales de Côte-d'Ivoire* – National Armed Forces of Ivory Coast) recapture in the aftermath.

The operation is a success, but it demonstrates that the rebels have weapons and know how to use them. Another observation: these new adversaries opposed to the democratically elected government of Laurent Gbagbo know how to maneuver and fight at night, which is rather rare in Africa.

The Rebels and Mutineers Enjoy a Wind in their Sails

On another front, the government troops realize the ability of the rebels at great expense. On 29 November, with the support of white mercenaries and supported by two Mi-24 "Hind" attack helicopters, the confident FANCI make a move to recapture Vavoua. The choice of this objective is a sensible one because it allows Daloa, the cocoa capital of the world, to be shielded against attack. It also separates the MPCI from the two new rebel movements in the west.

A first wave of 4x4 vehicles filled with soldiers and supported by an ERC-90, a BMP-2, and a VLRA armed with 20mm cannon advances on the straight road and reaches the suburbs of the town. The command element follows with a second wave, but is ambushed by men under the

The groupe de combat (combat group), which is equivalent to a US squad, is armed with specific weapons. Two of them are a FR-F2 sniper rifle and a 5.56mm Minimi LMG, such as the one carried by the paratrooper in the foreground.

Paratroopers of 4th Company of the 1st RCP patrol in the bush near Brobo. In any type of guerilla war, it is important to clear away foliage alongside the main roads to reduce the threat of an ambush. The solider walking point carries a FR-F2 sniper rifle.

command of staff sergeant Codé Zacharias as they return down the road. A FANCI major is killed, which signals a stampede. Threatened with encirclement, the first wave has to force a passage to reach its base of departure. In the fray, two white mercenaries are seriously wounded and a rocket destroys the BMP. In the eastern part of the country, the rebels attack the villages of Sorobango and Koutougba to the north of Bondoukou. The press totally ignores these skirmishes.

This series of engagements proves that as the Christmas holidays approach the cease-fire is not being respected and, due to the limited number of troops involved, Operation Unicorn is unable to control a front of more than 800 km (500 miles). On the other side, the position of the rebels has been strengthened. Three months after the events of 19 September, they control half of the country, which the regular army seems unable to recapture.

The opening of a new front in the west and the appearance of two new rebel groups would be a surprise to the French political leaders who, after the fall of Man, reinforced Operation Unicorn. The nightmare of a rebel breakthrough at San Pedro harbor and the collapse of the FANCI would appear to sound the death knell of the remaining economic miracle of Ivory Coast. Added to that is the risky evacuation of the 60,000 nationals in Abidjan (1) right in the middle of the holidays, which would cause the credibility of the French policy in Africa to suffer.

Reinforcements for Unicorn

In the aftermath, the 1st and 4th Companies of the 2nd REP arrive. The 1st Company is immediately sent to Guessabo to effect a blockade at

(1)   The government of Ivory Coast intends to arm a people's army consisting of 20,000 young people without any military experience – a real potential nightmare for any operation in the megalopolis of Abidjan where there certainly exists a rebel fifth column.

Paratroopers of the 4th Company, 1st RCP stand watch in a street in Borobo. The attitude of the population ethnically close to the rebels changed after the reinforcement of Operation Unicorn in mid-December.

The MPCI accuses the French of supporting the government offensive and trying to stop the rebel advance. It is clear that if the French Army had not been deployed in October, Abidjan would have quickly been captured by the rebels.

the front in the west, while the 4th is kept in reserve for the Toumodi theatre. Other reinforcements are expected to arrive by sea by the end of the year (2). This makes Unicorn the largest operation led by the French Army in Africa since Operation Manta in Chad.

In Abidjan, the press, who seem to have forgotten the violent anti-French campaign of last October, present the French reinforcement as a commitment of the French Republic for the side of the government forces. This may be a little premature, however, since the mission of the soldiers engaged in Operation Unicorn remains unchanged from the three original main goals:

1) Protect the nationals. On this point, the Secretary of State for foreign affairs, Renaud Muselier, has made it clear: "Not a question. No one touches a single hair of a Frenchman in Ivory Coast."

2) Freeze the military situation to allow a negotiated solution to the crisis.

3) Protect the civilian population with the threat of opening fire if there are any acts of violence.

At the command post of General Beth located in the 43rd BIMa in Abidjan, even vocabulary has adapted to the new situation. They speak of "mutineers" when referring to the people of the MPCI who, in theory, signed the cease-fire and they use the word "rebels" when discussing the partisans in the MPIGO and the MJP.

(2)   It consists of a company of the 8th RPIMa from the EEI-2 (*escadron d'éclairage et d'investigation* – reconnaissance and investigation squadron – of the 2nd DB), a 120mm-mortar battery, and ALAT and logistic elements.

Stone Rain at Borobo

Though the government at Abidjan seems to be relatively satisfied, the atmosphere at Bouaké, the rebel capital, has become openly anti-French. During a demonstration, the GCP (*Groupe Commando Parachutiste* – Pathfinders) of Major Courcelles had to fire into the air in order to disengage, while the 4th Company of the 1st REP used tear gas to scatter a hostile crowd.

Farther east, at the collection point, the section under the adjutant Guerin occupies Borobo. At night, the "grays" (who were nicknamed after the color of their scarves) of the 4th observe the surroundings at the small

General view of the HQ of the 3rd Company of 1st RCP in Tiébessous. Note the presence of two armored cars of the 1st RIMa (Régiment d'Infanterie de Marine – Naval Infantry Regiment), which is a light armored car formation equipped with Sagaie ERC-90s.

Front view of the turret of an ERC-90 armored car of 1st RIMa seen in Tiébessous. From this position, these vehicles destroyed two Toyotas full of rebels at the start of the events last October.

Paratroops of the 3rd Company of 1st RCP help to dislodge a bogged down P-4. Deployment in Africa is popular among the troops, especially the young paras, who can have an adventure while gaining experience in the field.

Attached to this FAMAS assault rifle is a red beret and the standard of the 3rd Company of the 1st RCP deployed in Africa. The baby python wrapped around the weapon was a gift from the rebels.

village through a Sophie thermal camera. The robust non-commissioned officer declared to us, "The atmosphere has changed. The village, which is 98% favorable to us, is afraid. Agitators have infiltrated. Yesterday my Peugeot P-4 4x4 was stoned."

To the south, the paratroopers of Colonel Thuet, the commanding officer of the 1st REP, has a solid hold on Tiébessou, the bolt of the Yamoussoukro road, the spiritual capital of the country.

An engineer section of the 6th RG (*Régiment de Génie* – Engineer Regiment) built a mini-Maginot Line northwest of the village. The people under Captain Joussen-Anglade occupy virtual bunkers strengthened by enormous logs of tropical wood. For the moments relations are cordial between the red berets and the FANCI and mutineers. These latter offered to the captain a baby python, while the government troops gave him a puppy.

"On the mutineer's side," says a non-commissioned officer, "the base is excited and the young people defy the authority of the leaders who would like to see a political solution to the problem. In the region of Sakassou, the 'Robin Hood' myth of the MPCI is collapsing due to the violence. The FANCI, aware that the French are here, are beginning to leave this front to reinforce the west. It is risky to stay here for very long."

Other French soldiers have held their position for more than a month.

These include the Legionnaire parachutists of the CEA of the 2nd REP commanded by Captain Doucet. The company participated in the evacuation of westerners from Man before monitoring the attempt made by the FANCI to retake Vavoua.

Massacre Avoided at Banouflé

On Saturday, 21 December, troops were called to battle stations. To protest the new French politics, the youth of Vavoua are marching to the Legionnaire positions to appeal to France. Captain Doucet is worried. He would have doubtless preferred to engage in real combat rather than supervise a volatile crowd that could quickly become impossible to control.

At the checkpoint, two combat groups are in position. A band of cartridges is loaded in the 12.7mm machine gun and a missile has been secured in the Milan post. Four Legionnaire paratroops are sent forward on the straight road to indicate to the demonstrators the line they cannot cross. One hundred meters to the rear, a 7-man combat team led by a NCO of British origin blocks the road.

From the bunker crowning the checkpoint, the Milan crewman observes through his optics the place where the road disappears at the crest of the opposite side of the hill.

"Here they are!" he cries. "They're running down the hillside." The

The light Marmont truck is obsolete in Europe but it is still used efficiently in Ivory Coast. Note that a large log was placed across the trail to create an obstacle in case of government attack.

From their position in Banouflé (which is midway between Daloa and Vavoua), a combat group of the CEA of the 2nd REP observes the advance of a large crowd during a demonstration on 20 December. The Legionnaire in the foreground near the truck has two rifle grenades in his belt. A FR-F2 sniper rifle team has set up their position in the background. The truck is the famous VLRA, which is especially well adapted to the bush.

This bunker was built at the French position north of Daloa. The Legionnaires are on full alert since there are only 25 of them facing a crowd of 3000 that includes young guerillas.

terrain masks a part of the demonstrators, but they become more and more numerous until they darken the side of the hill. "One thousand . . . Two thousand . . . They keep on coming, Lieutenant!"

Several minutes later, the officer calls the captain on the radio. "Blue from Blue 1. A crowd of an estimated 3500 persons is 500 meters [550 yards] from my position." The Legionnaire paratroops number about 20. Tension is high. The breeze carries the clamoring of the demonstrators. Captain Doucet arrives in his P-4 4x4 and goes to meet with Codé Zacharias, whose warriors make up the head of the column. Some of them are very excited and aim their PPSh- 43s at the four Legionnaires while passing their fingers across their throats in a threatening gesture. The Legionnaires do not falter but keep their fingers curled over the triggers of their FAMAS. The captain, who warns the rebel leader against any trouble, receives the message to restore order before going back to his CP.

The four lone Legionnaires facing the hostile crowd receive the order to fall back to the combat group's gathering point. A British NCO prepares for the worst because the head of the demonstration seems to be taken with convulsions. "Zacharias is having a hard time controlling twenty hotheads," the corporal realizes. "In case of firing," he orders, "don't hit the ground without orders. For the *lacrymo* [tear gas grenade], drop immediately. Open fire only on command." (3)

Suddenly, two 4x4 vehicles armed with a 14.5mm machine gun and filled with rebels appear on the crest and split the crowd as they head for the leader of the demonstration. The Legionnaires hold their breath. The

(3)   The legionnaires often wait a second before throwing a grenade so it cannot be tossed back at them. Such a pause is not necessary with a tear gas grenade.

A Milan post is at the ready in the French bunker. This weapon can be used if a rebel 4x4 vehicle tries to attack the position. The range and the road's configuration are perfect, but the Milan cannot be fired against a crowd.

The captain commanding the CEA of the 2nd REP watches to see how the situation plays out during the demonstration. Note the badge of the 2nd REP on the windscreen and the three small flags on the antenna: the national flag, the red and green flag of the Legion, and the dark blue colors of the CEA company. The machine gun is an AN-F-1, a 7.62mm NATO version of the AA-52 used during the war in Algeria.

This photograph shows the intimidating appearance of the pro-rebel crowd during the demonstration south of Vavoua.

This NCO has a smile on his face despite the seriousness of the situation. Legionnaire paras are very well trained and motivated. Being in action is the purpose of their life. It is interesting to see how the Legionnaire parachutists are equipped at the beginning of the 21st century. Note the flak jacket.

rebels disembark and, using their gun butts, calm the young hotheads. "Zacharias has launched his Guard," a relieved lieutenant states simply.

Hussar Parachutists and Legionnaires under Fire

At the same time, 100 kilometers west of the position of the CEA, another company of the 2nd REP is under fire, and this time it's for real. After the rebels recaptured Man on 18 December, Colonel Maurin, commander of the 2nd REP, restructured his troops. On 18 December, the 1st Company receives the order to leave Guessabo and to cross the Sassandra River to hold Doukou, an important crossroads of

The largest attack on this position took place on 6 January when rebels supported by RPG-7s and 81mm mortars tried to overrun the bunker. One VAB was hit on the left door by an RPG-7 grenade and the driver lost an arm.

Troops belonging to the 1st Company of the 2nd REP operate the checkpoint northwest of Doukou. This position was attacked several times between 20 December and the first days of January 2003. One weapon used to defend the spot is a .50 caliber machine gun.

communication. The 4th Company will secure the axis between Doukou and Guessabo, where Colonel Maurin sets up the CP of the REP. Doukou, held by Captain Dunant's 1st Company, is henceforth the westernmost extremity of the French lines. The town exudes fear. The MPIGO, which includes in its ranks numerous Liberian looters, does not have the reputation of the MPCI among the civilian population. As for the FANCI, themselves terrorized by the rebels, they fire at everything that moves and hold the population hostage.

Captain Dunant warned his Legionnaires well. All rebel attacks will be met with unmeasured retaliation and, furthermore, any member of the FANCI who threatens a civilian will be arrested. If a government soldier kills a civilian, they will open fire. The captain oversees his men from his command post set up in the city school.

On the outskirts of town, his sections of Legionnaire paratroopers control the asphalt axes that lead to Man in the northwest and to Guiglo and Bloékin in the southwest. The 1st platoon of the 1st Squadron of the 1st RHP (*Régiment de Huassards Parachutistes*), nicknamed "111", is attached to the company with three ERC-90 Sagaies and three VBLs. They watch the trail in the northeast that leads to Kouibli. Rumors spread about a lot of rebels infiltrating on foot into this zone. As for the FANCI, they seem to be in trouble on the Guiglo-Bloékin axis and in Bangolo where the rebels are gaining ground. To avoid being surrounded in the middle of nowhere, the 1st Company and the hussar parachutists increase the number of patrols. They cannot count on the FANCI bunched together on the road with their T-55 and BMP.

On 19 December, Bangolo falls into the hands of the rebels. The FANCI are a bit beaten up and they leave thirty of their men on the ground. The lack of fighting spirit among the government troops is made worse by the fact that the rebels show no mercy; fifty-seven wounded government

During the fight, which raged for three hours, nine Legionnaires were wounded and 30 rebels were killed. In the background of this photo is an ERYX light missile launcher.

A platoon from the 1er Hussard Parachutiste Regiment is attached to the 1st Company of the 2nd REP. The platoon is composed of three VBLs and three ERC-90 Sagaies.

soldiers would end up in the hospital at Man. From that point the rebels are only about 20 kilometers (12 miles) from the checkpoint northwest of Doukou. At dawn on the 20th, the mists of Harmattan (Ivorian winter) rise above a terrified village.

Intelligence gathered by aircraft from the Bréguet Atlantic confirms that the rebels are moving toward the city. At 1330 (1:30 p.m.), Captain Dunant is on the march with the Sagaies *Sebastopol* and *Phillipsburg* (4) supported by two VBLs that control the northeast access to the city. In the turret, the young officer commanding the platoon, Lieutenant Lafontaine, observes with his binoculars the red-colored laterite in the straight roads leading toward Blodi.

(4)   French armored vehicles often have the name of a battle painted on the hull.

Suddenly, a red Mercedes appears from behind the crest 1500 meters (1640 yards) away, speeding down the road. The captain orders a warning shot. From the turret of the *Sepastopol*, an ANF-1 machine gun spits a burst. The Mercedes continues to charge while one of the rebels shoulders an RPG-7 as he positions himself in the open roof of the car. Another rebel fires a short burst from a Kalashnikov without effect. A second burst has no more success than the first. The car is now only 700 meters (765 yards) from the French lines.

"Fire for effect!" yells the captain. Lieutenant Lafontaine and the crew of the other Sagaie disappear into the turret. The 90mm tube thunders and a high-explosive shell explodes just in front of the Mercedes. In a cloud of dust, the damaged Mercedes sways then runs off the road into a ditch. At the same time, two 4x4s filled with rebels comes tearing around the bend, rolling side by side, spraying small arms fire. The two armored

The VBL shown here was photographed northeast of Doukou where rebels launched their first attack on 20 December.

This is one of the ERC-90 Sagaies that destroyed the red Mercedes that threatened the French position.

cars fire a new salvo of HE shells while the 12.7mm on the VBL blazes away. A few moments later, seven shells pulverize the rebel vehicles, but the captain knows there are still seven more 4x4s behind the crests.

Discouraged by this setback and unwilling to press the attack, the rebels fall back, leaving behind a weak rear guard that ties up the Legionnaires for a few minutes. The arrival of two Gazelle helicopters armed with 20mm guns causes them to scatter into the brush. Except for a camouflage-clad corpse in the Mercedes, the rebels left no dead or wounded behind. Captain Dunant estimates the number of rebel casualties to be "5 or 6."

The initial attempt at a reconnaissance in force failed. At the time of this writing, however, three subsequent skirmishes have pitted the rebels against the Legionnaires and the hussar parachutists, fortunately without loss. But on 29 December, two 81mm mortars positioned at the school intervene to support an ambushed patrol. This series of clashes demonstrates that the rebels are feeling the effect of French activity around Doukou.

A serious confrontation occurs on 6 January 2003. In the middle of the afternoon, rebels of the MPIGO simultaneously attack two checkpoints. Mortars and RPG-7s are used to support the assault. During the course of the battle, which lasts for two hours, 30 rebels are killed and 9 French soldiers are wounded.

If the rebels manage to inflict a major defeat on the FANCI on the Bloekin-Guiglo road, the French Army will definitely be first in line and choices will have to be made. The Paris Match newspaper quoted Codé Zachariah, who summarized perfectly the situation: "The Frenchmen deal with us because they are afraid that Gbagbo will fall and they support him a lot in case he stays. In this kind of game, you risk losing everything."

For a while, peace returns to the northeast checkpoint at Doukou. The two Sagaie vehicles are still in position. Lieutenant Lafontaine, who has come down from his turret, observes the refugees pouring from Man. A poor, resigned population that has been looted by the Liberians, they have lost everything. Among the throng is a young lady. Situated as he is on the opposite side of the turret, the young officer does not notice that she has

The "111" (1st platoon, 1st Squadron of the 1st RHP) was tasked with watching the red-earth trail northwest of Doukou when the rebels attacked.

A decrepit Mercedes sits abandoned on the side of the road after being destroyed by an ERC-90 when it tried to assault the French position.

Engineers from the 6th RG (Régiment de Génie – Engineer Regiment) prepare to dispose of an unexploded RPG-7 rocket.

Profile view of the engineer version of the VAB armored vehicle. On top of the vehicle are road obstacles used at checkpoints.

only a stump in place of a right hand – a "short cut", the signature of the rebels of Sierra Leone. They seem to have found a new theatre of operation. If nothing is done, the economic miracle of Ivory Coast will be only a beautiful memory and the Pearl of West Africa will sink into darkness.

Mercenaries in the Conflict

The conflict in Ivory Coast has attracted mercenaries into the two camps. Natives of Burkina Faso side with the mutineers, while the MPIGO have the support of the Liberians and the remnants of the bands of the RUF of the sinister Fode Sanko. These troops often consist of child-soldiers who are on drugs, drunk on alcohol and of generally poor character, who have been fighting for years in Liberia and Sierra Leone. They are financed by the diamond dealers who are using the chaos of war to exploit the rich deposits in the region where these new "big companies" are spreading their terror. The western part of Ivory Coast, which is being saved as a reserve for future generations by the father of the nation, Houphouet-Boigny, contains numerous potential mineral resources. If the situation continues as it has been, the region risks being quickly looted by the bands that have already sacked Man.

Sources have confirmed the arrival in the north of a team of black South Africans tasked with forming cadres and specialists in the MPCI. The rumor has not been confirmed, but the presence of portable SAM-7 missiles in the ranks of the rebels seems more than likely. At present, the rebels would not have the competence to use them, but certain lessons of the past should not go unheeded. At the end of the 1970s, half of the Portuguese aircraft at Guinea-Bissau were brought down in flames by the introduction of the SAM-7 "Strella" into the conflict. In Angola, the UNITA managed to shoot down several attack helicopters by conducting virtual anti-aircraft ambushes.

The use of mercenaries in the ranks of the government troops has resulted in the use of a lot of ink – and not always advisedly – by the international press. Reference was made at the beginning of the crisis of 500 Angolans, a figure that was wildly exaggerated. It is nevertheless likely that about 50 Angolans serve in positions of technical support for the BMPs and T-55s that Angola furnished to Ivory Coast.

This photo shows the front view of the engineer VAB. Note the road obstacles rising up behind the soldiers like spears.

French engineers from the 6th RG use a MPG (Moyen Polyvalent du Génie – Multi-purpose Engineer Tool), a large wheeled bulldozer, to build a bunker in Tiébessous.

A Transall C-160 lands at the airstrip in Vavoua. The Transall is particularly well suited for landing in the bush.

Members of the crew of this Gazelle armed with a 20mm gun, which belongs to the 5th RHC (Régiment d'Helicoptère de Combat), give the helicopter a final inspection prior to their mission.

Several times since the beginning of the crisis in Ivory Coast, Gazelle helicopters have been fired on and returned fire. One of the choppers was hit, but it sustained no serious damage.

Of course, it is the white mercenaries who are the big scoop for the press, particularly the team of mostly white South African pilots. These men pilot the Mi-24 "Hind" helicopters with the shark-mouth design seen in Yamoussoukro and Daloa. Two teams of Ukrainians and Byelorussians, who are not really known for their efficiency, maintain the "choppers." "JJ", a French pilot who at Yamoussoukro made a successful one-wheel landing of a Cessna reconnaissance aircraft that was as full of holes as a sieve, put together a team of Ivorian gunsmiths that performs their job pretty well. The pilot told us: "There is too much of a tendency to criticize the FANCI. We shouldn't forget that before the conflict, this Ivorian army, which had never been under fire, was the poor relation of the country. Daily these men find themselves in combat without any experience."

The other group of mercenaries, the "ground force", must doubtless think the same. Like the reverses suffered by the FANCI show, the training will be long and painful. The group of mercenaries, some of which are from "Denard's gang" (5), are the "volunteer firemen" of Ivory Coast. The press will criticize the group as a bunch of supermarket vigilantes in camouflage clothing who are supervised by a 50-year-old NCO and who don't have a chance of gaining a victory. Here again the criticism is too easy to make. These people have pulled off a series of minor miracles. Lacking real logistics and organization, these totally inexperienced African soldiers, who have never had time to train, are thrown into battle in small groups against substantially superior firepower to merely delay the inevitable.

One of their leaders testifies over the telephone: "The Mi-8s piloted by the Bulgarians can no longer approach the front to evacuate the

wounded because the firing is so intense. You have to imagine the number of rockets fired by the rebels to destroy a single BMP. This proves that there are vast logistics involved. But each rocket fired at us is one that will not be fired at the soldiers of Unicorn."

Another observation: During a Mi-24 raid between Vavoua and Man, a virtual depot of fuel and munitions would have been destroyed. This contradicts the image of a rebellion of disorganized barefoot ruffians. Most of the foreign volunteers believe there is a strong financial power behind the rebels.

The front is a dangerous place. Already several mercenaries have been seriously wounded. "We are no longer the Africa of the de-colonization era, when a handful of mercenaries would scatter a horde of Africans armed with *poupou* rifles (6)," another leader stated, "but the ideal of the old days lives on. We are fighting for a certain concept of Africa. Taylor could offer us a golden bridge, but we still wouldn't be on his side. Even if it has flaws, the legal government of Ivory Coast must be defended. If it falls, that's the end of France's credibility in Africa."

At the time of this writing, the city of Nake, near the port of Taboo, had just fallen into the hands of the rebels who have no doubt come straight from Liberia. This new victory put San Pedro in their reach and opens a new front that further splits up the country. Further, the MPCI is threatening to violate the cease-fire. A new defeat for the FANCI would more than likely place the French Army in the front lines opposite the rebels.

(5) Bob Denard was a famous French mercenary who fought in Katanga, Yemin, Benin, Comoro, and other locations.

(6) *Poupou* rifle — A contraband rifle dating from the 19th century used in the African conflicts of the beginning of the 1970s.

Puma helicopters from the 3rd RHC have been used in Ivory Coast for troop transport and Medevac flights.

Puma helicopters have remained in service for a long time. The Puma is to be updated prior to the arrival of the NH-90 in 2008.

This photograph of the famous Mi-24 "Hind" helicopter that the mercenary pilots fly was taken clandestinely by the author; he spent a day retained by government troops for taking it.

Mi-24 helicopters have been the cause of a large number of casualties on the rebel side.

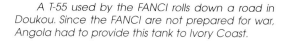

A T-55 used by the FANCI rolls down a road in Doukou. Since the FANCI are not prepared for war, Angola had to provide this tank to Ivory Coast.

A T-55 operated by FANCI soldiers advances toward the rebels. Military training is slow and difficult for the Ivorian troops.

Swift, Silent and Deadly
USMC Force Recon
Joel B. Paskauskas II

A CRCC or "rubber duck" is useful for riverine insertions such as depicted here. In these small, versatile boats, Force Recon Marines can ride in from over the horizon with a very small radar signal that hopefully the enemy mistakes for sea clutter. (Yves Debay)

In the summer of 1957 the first company of Force Reconnaissance marines stood to at Camp Pendleton in California. They can trace their heritage to the Amphibious Recon Battalions and Companies formed in World War II. The Force Recon companies eventually found themselves in the Republic of Vietnam, where they served with distinction. Forty-four Marine and Sailors assigned to the 1st Force Recon, never made it home and some are still listed as missing in action. Force Recon Marines have been involved in numerous other operations in Liberia, Somalia and Operation Desert Shield/Storm. In fact it was a group of Force Recon Marines that were the first coalition troops to enter Kuwait City and subsequently liberate the American Embassy.

This book intends to profile in pictures and words on the current missions and equipment of marines that make up the Force Recon Companies in today's United States Marine Corps. It should be noted about some of the major differences between Recon and Force Recon. As one Recon Marine explained it to the author, the major difference is "mileage and perspective." Recon battalions work in support of division intelligence gathering out to approximately ten miles beyond the forward edge of the battle area (FEBA). Whereas Force Recon companies gather intel beyond this 10-mile limit and support the Marine Expeditionary Force (MEF) which is equivalent to an Army Corps. Force Recon marines are trained in more complicated insertion means, such as HALO, SCUBA and SPIE. Another Force Recon Marine described it this way "Force Recon works for the Marine Expeditionary Unit commander and the Recon Battalions work for the battalion commanders."

PT or physical training is an intergral part of any Marines daily routine, especially for Force Recon Marines. Candidates for Force Recon must score a 275 out of a possible 300 on the Marine Corps PFT or Physical Fitness Test. (Yves Debay)

These Marines from the 2nd Force Reconnaissance Company are participating in the Swiss Raid competition in Neufchatel, Switzerland.

Pedal power, going to war Swiss-style. These Force Recon operators are riding bikes while wearing burdensome ALICE packs in route to their next mission.

Interestingly enough Force Recon certainly tries to maintain a very low profile. The Marine Corps strives not to create the notion of an elite force within an elite force. Force Recon missions, like the missions of Special Forces Operation Detachment Delta, seldom see the light of publicity or public record. In the Marine Corps today there are three Force Recon companies. One is a stand-alone unit, the 1st Force Reconnaissance Company. 1st Force Recon was established in June of 1957 and can trace its heritage to the Fleet Marine Force Pacific (FMFPAC) Amphibious Reconnaissance Company. And depending on whom you talk to, it is considered to be the senior Force Recon unit in the Corps.

The other two Force Recon Companies are part of the 2nd

To bear any burden. Participating in these international commando competitions allows Force Recon Marines to interact with their brother special operators and hone a variety of commando, war-fighting skills.

Reconnaissance Battalion based at Camp Lejeune, North Carolina and the 3rd Reconnaissance Battalion based in Okinawa. 2nd Force Recon was formed in June of 1958. It was birthed out of the ranks of the Fleet Marine Force Atlantic Amphibious Reconnaissance Company. There are also two Marine Corps Reserve Force Recon companies, one in Mobile, Alabama the 3rd Force Reconnaissance Company. And the other, 4th Force Reconnaissance Company at the Marine Corps Base at Kaneohe Bay, Hawaii, which has a detachment in Reno, Nevada. The 5th Force Recon Company was recently deactivated.

Force Recon companies is made up of 85 highly trained marines, divided into an HQ, a supply and service platoon and six separate Recon platoons. In each platoon there are three, four man teams. Their stated missions are: intelligence gathering, close with and destroy the enemy, implant sensors, capture selected prisoners, and conduct specialized terrain reconnaissance. Until recently Force Recon Companies had not been part of the United States Special Operations Command (USSOCOM). But recent events and the war on terrorism have necessitated their integration into USSOCOM and Force Recon will be part of this unified command. During the formation of SOCOM in the late 1980's the Marine Corps elected to remain apart from that command. Instead the Marine Corps forged ahead with a plan to train their Marine Expeditionary Units to a level known as Special Operation Capable.

Force Recon Marines are tasked with two primary mission profiles. In the parlance of Force Marines, they are known as "black" and "green." Green refers to their more "conventional" (if you can call what Force Recon does conventional) missions such as amphibious recon, deep ground recon as well as other surveillance operations. The other side of the coin, "black" missions involve GOPLAT, VBSS and other direct action type mission profiles. In order to be able to get where they are going to perform these black and green missions, Force Recon Marines have a wide array of means to accomplish this. By land they can use their Improved

Training in arctic or winter conditions is part of Force Recon's training regimen. The basic Force Recon unit is made up of six Marines usually led by a staff sergeant. A Force Recon platoon contains three team and is commanded by a lieutenant. (DoD)

Fast Attack Vehicles, which are a Mercedes-Benz product that can carry a crew of four and has a hard point in the back for a .50 caliber heavy machine gun or a Mk.19 40mm automatic grenade launcher. Motorcycles and Humm-vees are also at their disposal. The Force Recon companies have in the past used Chenowth Light Strike Vehicles, but these have since been retired. If is by air they want to deploy, you name it and they do it. HALO, HAHO, SPIE (Special Purpose Insertion/Extraction) and FRIES (Fast Rope Insertion/Extraction System) are just some of the ways these operators can deploy. When it comes to waterborne insertion, they are experts at this as well. They can deploy from subs, ships, SCUBA, sub-surface with Dräger re-breathers, and several other ways.

So you want to be a Force Recon Marine? Think twice after you read the selection process. Only the brave and the bold need apply. Any Marine regardless of their job, or Military Occupational Specialty (MOS) as it is known in military parlance may apply. Generally Marines with a strong infantry background are prime candidates. But keep in mind, at the core of the Marine ethos, is the fact that no matter what job they may hold, every Marine is a rifleman at heart. Force Recon looks for Marines that are both mentally and physically suited for the job, good shooters and strong swimmers. To even be considered for Force Recon, candidates must pass an evaluation similar to Ranger Indoctrination Program (RIP) or the Special Forces Assessment School (SFAS) that are conducted by the Army. The Force Recon indoctrination begins with a PFT (Physical Fitness Test), an obstacle course, a 10-mile run in combat boots with a rifle and rucksack, a psychological screening and a personal subject interview with a tough-as-nails Force Recon Sergeant Major. A very small percentage actually passes this initial indoctrination course.

Recovery of downed aviators, like this one featured here, is a mission that Force Recon stands ready to do should the need arise.

Navy Corpsmen assigned to Force Reconnaissance Companies are highly trained special operations medics. All have attended the difficult "18D" special ops medic course at Fort Bragg, North Carolina.

This Force Recon Operator is equipped with a full size M16A2. The M16A2 is the standard battle rifle for the Marine Corps. He wears Nomex aviator's gloves that have had the fingertips removed. Also his BDU's are sterile, meaning no rank, nametapes or branch of service identifiers. (Alberto Scarpitta)

Sitting on his ALICE pack, this Force Recon Marine takes a well-earned brake during a training mission. Note the M4/M203 close at hand. (Alberto Scarpitta)

Once the Marine is accepted into the company, he begins an extensive, arduous training evolution that begins with an eight week long basic recon course that is conducted at the Naval Amphibious Base at Little Creek, Virginia on the east coast or NAB Coronado, California on the west coast. Here the Marine hones his skills as a recon operator. This is the start of Phase One individual training. From there the Marine travels to the Combatant Dive Course at Panama City, Florida. No time for tanning on the beach here, as during the ensuing eight-weeks, the Marine will learn all about open and closed circuit diving, dive physics and medicine and various other topics related to combat diving.

After eight weeks at Panama City, the Marine travels to Fort Benning, Georgia, for a basic airborne school that lasts three weeks. Upon completion, he will be awarded his jump wings and will have made five static line jumps. After this, the Marine will be afforded the opportunity to attend a variety of specialty schools, such as the Military Free Fall (MFF) in Yuma, Arizona, and the U.S. Army Ranger School, also at Fort Benning, just to name a few.

It should be mentioned that Navy Corpsmen provides vital medical support to Force Recon Companies. Corpsmen also undertake a demanding 72-week training cycle that includes the first three schools mentioned above that Force Recon Marines undertake. After that advanced special operations medics courses offered at Fort Bragg are also part of their training package. At the end, these highly trained corpsmen are both providers of advanced medical care and fully trained operators and shooters.

Phase Two of a Force Recon Marine focuses on building the platoon into cohesive fighting unit. This portion begins when all the operators have

This Force Recon operator relays some vital information via a satellite radio during a NATO training exercise. Note the ever popular "boonie hat". Recently it has been decided that Force Recon shall officially become part of the Joint Special Operations Command or JSOC. (Alberto Scarpitta)

All Force Recon Marines like those pictured here attend the Marine Corps Combatant Diver Course at Panama City, Florida. In addition to the Combatant Diver Course, all Force Recon operators must complete a 12-week Basic Reconnaissance Course. (Yves Debay)

completed the basic qualification courses. One of the primary objectives of this phase is to allow the operators to come together and put into practice all that they have learned over the past several months. They will conduct deep reconnaissance and amphibious missions together. Several courses are integral to this portion of Force Recon platoons training. They will attend advanced communications schools, shoot thousands of .45 ACP and 5.56mm rounds, conduct force-on-force missions using Simmuniton paint marking cartridges, and other team building exercises and missions. They will familiarize themselves with the enemy's weapons, learn how to call in devastating air and naval gunfire as well as close in air support (CAS). Other topics covered in Phase Two include more HAHO training, amphibious training and use of the Dräger LAR-V closed circuit-breathing apparatus in infiltration ops. Combat life saving techniques are reinforced to enable Force Recon Marines to care for their fallen comrades often while under fire. Phase Two ends with several full blown training exercises in various climates that allow the Marines to utilize all their skills in a realistic environment, as real as you can get without going to war.

At the end of Phase Two, the platoon is locked and loaded and good to go. At this point they have been operating together for a period of six months. The six-month final phase of their training is conducted under the watchful hands of seasoned senior non-commissioned officers assigned to the Special Operations Training Group (SOTG). SOTG's prime mission is to further prep the team for deployment as part of a MEU(SOC). The MEU (SOC) is a forward deployed joint Marine unit that is tasked to perform special maritime operations. The MEU (SOC) is really the tip of the spear when it comes to an American presence anywhere in the world. A MEU (SOC) is made up of a Command Element (CE), Ground Combat Element (GCE), Aviation Combat Element (ACE) and a Combat Service Support Element (CSSE).

The tip of the tip of the spear within the MEU (SOC) is the Maritime Special Purpose Force (MSPF). This element is staffed primarily with Force Recon Marines but is also supported by other elements of the MEU. Supporting the MSPF mission is the primary task that Force Recon supports presently. The MSPF gives the MEU commander the ability to

Operating in a littoral or coastal maritime environment is within the scope of missions for Force Recon. (Yves Debay)

The CRCC as picture here can carry up to six fully equipped Marines. It can also be sub-surface deployed from a submarine.

This Force Recon Marine is carefully guiding his Zodiac boat off of a Navy ship. This Zodiac will support helocast ops by recovery swimmers.

Breaking through the crest of a wave, these Marines steer their CRCC back to the mother ship.

conduct special missions such as recon and surveillance, specialized demolitions, GOPLAT (gas oil platform) seizure/recovery operations, and rescue and recovery of selected personnel and sensitive equipment, VBSS (visit, board, search and seizure) ops and tactical recovery of aircraft and personnel (TRAP).

The SOTG will run the platoon through a series of courses covering such topics as Close Quarters Battle (CQB), explosive entry and urban sniper ops. The final exam, if you will for the platoon and other elements of the MSPF is the TRUEX. Training in Urban Environment Exercise is one of the major exercises a MEU (SOC) goes through prior to actual deployment. TRUEX is based on three separate scenarios that build on each other and become increasingly more complex and difficult.

Life for a Force Recon Marine centers on a cycle of training in preparation to be part of a MSPF on "float" somewhere in the world ready to support our National Command Authority. The Force Recon Marines that I had the pleasure of speaking with really see their job as one of supporting the "grunt" or Marine Infantryman, to enable him to know his enemy better, and then close with and destroy him. The only difference they see in themselves from the rest of the grunts out there is the means they use to get to work and tools they use when they get there.

I would like to thank the Marines of the 2nd Force Reconnaissance Company, especially Lt. Buffa and Gunny Bob Hall. Also thanks to my dear friends Robert and Steffanie Rentz. This book is dedicated to my favorite Marine, Lt. Colonel Rick Hey, Jr. USMC (Ret), my hero and true patriot. Thanks for instilling a deep and profound love for my country and flag. Semper Fidelis.

In this photo, a Phrog gives birth to a Duck. The Phrog is the nickname given to the venerable CH-46 Sea Knight and the duck is a soft rubber inflatable boat used by Force Recon Marines.

With fins in hand, this Marine leaps off the back deck of a CH-46 into the ocean below. This method of insertion is also known as helo casting.

The U.S. Naval Ship Leroy Grummar serves as a training ground for Force Recon Marines as they practice their boarding techniques.

These Force Recon Marines are conducting a VBSS mission. VBSS stands for Vessel Boarding Search and Seizure. Note the thick leather gloves attached to the Marines FSBE. These are used to prevent serious burns to the hands while fast roping.

Loving every minute of it. This Protec helmeted Force Recon Marine is obviously thoroughly enjoying the day's training missions.

Clearly focused on the task at hand, this Force Recon Marine wears his prescription glasses under his Bolle T-800 goggles. The Bolle T-800's are popular with U.S. specwar operators, but like all goggles, are subject to fogging up.

"Never leave a fellow comrade behind" is built into the warrior ethos of all Marines. This Marine bears the burden of a simulated casualty during a VBSS mission.

An excellent image of Force Recon Marines firing their MEUSOC .45 pistols. These pistols were introduced in 1985 and are immensely popular. Also note the six volt Surefire tactical lights.

Open circuit SCUBA diving as depicted here, is used by the Company only to support closed circuit diving training missions. The reason: SCUBA leaves a trace of bubbles, perfect for the enemy to track them. (Yves Debay)

After emerging from the water, the Sea Marines have removed their M4A1's from protective dry cases and are ready to snoop and poop. One operator's M4 is equipped with the quick detachable version of the M203 grenade launcher. The QD is part of the SOPMOD program for U.S. Special operations forces.

Emerging from the murky depths, these two Force Recon operators are ready for action. Note the M4A1 CQBW is equipped with an AN/PVS-17 MNVS. Their weapons would have been carried in secure dry bags.

Closed circuit is the preferred method for sub-surface swimming operations. They are equipped with the Norwegian made Dräger LAR-V re-breather. On the land it weighs 35 pounds but once in the water it is neutrally buoyant.

2nd Force Recon was formed in June 1958 from the Fleet Marine Force Atlantic amphibious reconnaissance company. It is the longest serving Force Recon Company in the Corps. It is based at Camp Lejeune, North Carolina.

Note the diving knife secured to the side of the LAR-V. The bottle beneath the main body of the Dräger holds about 13 cubic feet of oxygen at 2000 pounds per square inch.

The basic diving kit of the Force Recon Marine. The wet suit provides some buoyancy and insulation from the elements. On an actual operation, BDU's would be worn over these.

These two Force Recon Marines discuss the day's missions. The Marine in the foreground is armed with a M4/M203A1 combination. The M203 is a single shot, breech loading grenade launcher. (Alberto Scarpitta)

Beam us up Scotty! These Marines are equipped with satellite comms, as indicated by the folding antennas. Force Recon is equipped with the latest in high-tech comms gear. (Alberto Scarpitta)

Note the load bearing gear of this Force Reconnaissance Marine. Force Recon operators are allowed great leeway to modify their gear to fit their preferences and their changing operational needs. If they can't buy it from an outside source, usually somebody in the parachute shop can sew one up for them based on their design. (Alberto Scarpitta)

A fantastic shot of a Force Recon team fully rigged up on a SPIE operation. SPIE rigging is certainly not for the faint of heart. Fast roping is also a popular method of insertion, in fact it is the preferred method in some instances. (DoD)

Force Recon Marines get their first opportunity to put their knees in the breeze at the U.S. Army Airborne School at Fort Benning, Georgia. During their three weeks at Fort Benning, Marines make five static line jumps before they can earn their wings. The MC-1C low level static line parachute is the preferred static line parachute within the Force Recon companies. (Yves Debay)

These military free fallers are wearing the MC5 parachute. Using these heights maneuverable parachutes, they can travel silently for more than 50-kilometers after exiting the aircraft.

This Marine is ready for military free fall operations (MFF). Free fall Marines attend the MFF School at the U.S. Army Yuma Proving Ground at Yuma, Arizona. The Army cadre from this school is from B Company, 2nd Battalion, 1st SWTG (Special Warfare Training Group).

A front view of some of the kit worn by Force Recon free fallers. He wears the HGU-55/P helmet. This lightweight helmet is standard for all MFF ops. Considered to be one of the military's most demanding and potentially hazardous advanced skills, MFF ops are used to infiltrating enemy areas under cover of darkness and front great distances to avoid detection.

Safely secured and attached to his person, this CQBW is ready for action as soon as this marine hits the ground. An AN/PVS-17 Mini Night Vision Sight (MNVS) is attached to this M4A1.

The Force Recon Marines all wearing gear for a variety of MFF operations. They all wear Gore-Tex woodland camouflage jumpsuits. This is part of a kit designed specifically for MFF ops. It is called Parachute Individual Equipment Kit or PIEK.

Oxygen is a must for some MFF ops due to the altitudes. Here, attached to this operator's helmet is an MBU-12P pressure demand oxygen mask. Note the wrist-mounted MA2-30 military special ops altimeter.

Tandem Offset Release Delivery System or TORDS allows qualified military tandem jumpmasters to free fall parachute insertion with non-jump qualified personnel or up to 650 lbs. of gear. TORDS has two parts. The Military Vector Tandem System for personnel and the Military Tethered Bundle System for gear as illustrated here. When jumping with heavy loads, the jumper can carry the gear all the way down, lower it on a tether or release it and allow it to drop with its own chute.

Tandem jumping is wildly popular in civilian parachuting circles, but Force Recon has looked at its military uses and found that it has a place in their ops. By tandem jumping, they can insert with an individual who may not be jump qualified like a linguist or chemical expert.

Donning MFF gear is a two-man job. Here is an excellent view of the M6-S Static Line/Free-fall RAM Air Parachute System. It is unique to the USMC. It can be rigged for static line or MFF ops as the mission dictates.

Here, a group of Force Recon Marines fast rope out of the belly of an aged, but airworthy, CH-46 Sea Knight. Fast roping is the preferred method to get troops into restricted areas quickly and efficiently.

During the TRUEX exercises, all Marines involved get to experience what it's like working in a real city. The CH-46 pilots must fly low level in between buildings to deliver the Force Recon Marines on target.

These two Force Recon Marines help each other "jock-up" or suit-up prior to a mission. Note the blue magazines for the 1911A1 pistol that had been modified for use with Simmunition rounds. Force Recon Marines make up the assault portion of a Maritime Special Purpose Force.

This group of Force Recon Marines checks their communications equipment prior to an exercise near the end of the TRUEX. Note the blue barrels of their M4's, this indicates that are for sole use with the Simmunitions training rounds.

Listening intently to a pre-op briefing this Force Recon Marine is ready for action. An excellent view of the Modular Integrated Communications Helmet. Note the boom mike for the comm system as well as the Bolle T800 ballistic eyewear worn by this Force Recon Marine. The MICH or Modular/Integrated Communications Helmet is a vast improvement over the standard PASGT helmet. The MICH weighs only 3 pounds.

An interesting study of a Force Recon Marine. He is wearing the FSBE or Full Spectrum Battle Equipment or FSBE that has been specially designed for Force Recon use. The core of the FSBE is the Amphibious Assault Vest or AAV.

This Force Recon Marine has been specially trained and equipped to perform a wide variety of explosive entry techniques. The small pack he is donning contains all that he needs to take down a wide variety of doors and walls. These skills are learned from their peers at the Special Operations Training Group.

On any Force Recon mission you will find a Navy Corpsman. This special operations medics are some of the best trained and motivated in the world. He wears the MOLLE or Modular Lightweight Load Carrying Equipment Medics pack. MOLLE is an Army and Marine Corps item that replaces the aging ALICE (All-purpose, Lightweight, Individual Carrying Equipment) pack and Integrated Individual Fighting System introduced in 1988. MOLLE has had lots of problem since its introduction and is not popular with most Marines

Every aspect of an operation is rehearsed. Here Force Recon operators discuss how to handle non-combatants. The Marine on the right wears the recent issue Nomex Close Quarter Battle Assault Suit. This suit was designed to specifically meet the needs of Force Recon and various other special operations units. It differs from the standard Nomex CWU-27/P flight suit.

Breacher up! This operator is armed with a pistol gripped Remington 870 shotgun, with a 20" barrel. They are carried in a quiver on the marine's back or on a bungee attached to his load-bearing vest. Shotguns are used solely for breaching.

There is not an official Force Recon knife. It is largely left to the personal preference of the operator. This Force Recon Marine has chosen the excellent Mission MPK. These heavy-duty knives are lightweight titanium, immune to saltwater and chemicals. Strider custom-made knives are also immensely popular in the FR companies.

This Force Recon Marine is armed with a M4A1 SOPMOD carbine. This M4 is equipped with a visible light illuminator or VLI. Also note the thick gloves attached to his vest, these are for fastroping.

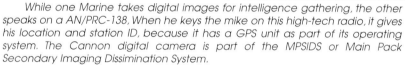

While one Marine takes digital images for intelligence gathering, the other speaks on a AN/PRC-138, When he keys the mike on this high-tech radio, it gives his location and station ID, because it has a GPS unit as part of its operating system. The Cannon digital camera is part of the MPSIDS or Main Pack Secondary Imaging Dissimination System.

This Marine, part of the MSPF Security Element, is packing a portable spike strip system on his back. It contains an accordion like system that, when opened, can be dragged across a street to deny access an area.

Some Force Recon Marines have attended Marine Scout Sniper as part of their training regimen. These scout snipers are an invaluable source of information. They use M40A1 sniper rifles that have served since their introduction in 1976. This bolt action rifle weighs 15 pounds and is chambered in 7.62mm NATO.

60

A close-up view of the MPSIDS. This system has two parts consisting of a laptop and printer and associated cables that make up the base station. The other portion is a camera and lenses and a palmtop computer. The Recon team can take pictures and send them via satellite radio for almost real time intelligence.

Here a Recon operator speaks on a AN/PRC138. This high frequency radio weighs about nine pounds without batteries! Not the foldable packable antenna.

Force Recon operators are afforded the discretion to use non-standard equipment. Sewing pockets to the upper sleeves of the BDU is a very functional modification. Sometimes Velcro is sewn to the top flap of these sleeve pockets to attach an American flag.

On patrol with Force Recon "Green" side ops include amphibious reconnaissance, deep ground reconnaissance, battlespace shaping and surveying the enemy to report their activities.

The M82A5 Special Application Scoped Rifle or SASR. This is a .50 caliber (12.7 x 99 mm) semi-automatic, air cooled magazine fed rifle. The scope is an Unertl Marine Sniper scope modified for use with this devastating weapon. The SASR's stated purpose is a long-range anti-material weapon, but it is also devastating when used against human beings. In a Force Recon company, there are ten of these in inventory.

The M249 Squad Automatic Weapon. One M249 SAW is carried per Recon team. This is the Para Model featuring a 13.5" barrel and a collapsible stock. It's fed from a 200-round disposable green plastic battle pack. The feed cover has a Milstd 1913 rail attached, which allows a variety of optical devices to be attached. It can also be jumped, meaning a Recon Marine can strap it to his body and leap out of an aircraft.

Putting on war paint, this Marine wears the Ranger Assault Carrying Kit or RACK. The RACK is patterned after the Chicom AK47 chest pouch, a design which, the Rhodesians and South Africans perfected.

On patrol with Force Recon. The Marine in the foreground is armed with the M4A1. Note the 30-round magazine has a length of paracord taped to the bottom. This improvised magazine pull aids the Marine to perform rapid magazine exchanges.

With the burning Kuwaiti oil fields in the background during Desert Storm, these Force Recon FAV's pause to resupply. The FAV's by some accounts were a

The FAV or Fast Attack Vehicle built by Chenowth saw use in Desert Storm by Force Recon. This is a derivative of a civilian off-road vehicle. It has now been replaced by the IFAV.

The IFAV or Interim Fast Attack Vehicle is a Mercedes Benz product that replaces the Chenowth FAV. It has a 90-horsepower engine that can propel it up to 80 mph. It is known commercially as the 290 SDT. The IFAV can be armed with a M2HB .50 caliber machine gun, an Mk.19 40mm automatic grenade launcher or a 7.62mm M240G machine gun. Its primary function is reconnaissance not attack, contrary to its name. The IFAV has a crew of three.

The KLR 250-D8 is a lightweight, rugged, commercial cross-country motorcycle that has been modified for military use. It is used for reconnaissance ops with the Recon BN and Force Recon companies. It has a range of 210 highway miles.

The tools of the trade from the simple, a sledge hammer, to the complex CQBW. The Full Spectrum Battle Equipment System (FSBE) incorporates a protective vest with hard plate armor and a single point release system.

The tack driving MEUSOC .45 pistol in a Safariland thermoplastic tactic al thigh holster.

These patches illustrate the recently decommissioned 5th Force Recon Company. Note the SCUBA 'bubble", the Pathfinder flaming torch, jump wings and paddles. All symbols of their ability to be swift, silent and deadly.

2nd Force Recon has seen action in the Dominican Republic, Lebanon and in the Persian Gulf. The cloth patch shown here is for novelty use only to be sewn on gym bags and shirts.

The breast insignia worn by Marines qualified in parachute and dive training are Force Recon Marine hallmarks. The gold wings are the Navy-Marine Parachutist badge. The SCUBA badge or "bubble" as it is affectionately known is the same worn by all SCUBA qualified U.S. military personnel.

The Marine Corps Close Quarter Battle Weapon. Note the blue barrel, denoting use of the SESAM or Special Effects Small Arms Martial System Kit. In common language, the SESAMS is known as Simmunition.

The FSBE with three 2 .30 round M16 magazine pouches. Note the pull ring at the shoulders. Should a Force Recon Marine find himself in the water, he could pull one of these rings and the panels would immediately separate, allowing him to escape.